Jim Pollard
The Kangaroo Kid

Praise from Jim Pollard's Colleagues and Competitors

"Jim Pollard was as close to the perfect basketball player as I ever had the pleasure of encountering. He was one of those rare athletes who made the game of basketball America's greatest game."

— *Bob Kurland, Hall of Famer (Oklahoma)*

"I think what impressed me the most was how easy he made it all look. Even as a young teenager I knew the game was tougher than that. While other players seemed to plod up and down the court Jim Pollard seemed to glide. I guess he could have been called the Fred Astaire of pro basketball. I have no doubt he'd have carried the same style, grace, and ease of performance into any sport he tried."

— *Hank Greenwald, Broadcaster*

"All I can tell you he was a great player. If playing today, he would be a superstar. Especially under the loose rules they now play."

— *Hank Luisetti, Hall of Famer, (Stanford)*

"Jim was a spectacular "individualist" who blended his skills to the team game (not easy with 'Big George' around) and produced the first great dynasty in this game we all love so much."

— *Bob Cousy, Hall of Famer (Boston)*

"Throughout his Hall of Fame career, Pollard demonstrated why his talents could easily transfer to today's game. Jim was the first player to really play the game "above the rim," where much of modern basketball is played."

— *George Mikan, Hall of Famer (Lakers)*

"Jim always handled himself with humility and was very popular with all those that played with him and against him. The more important the game the better Jim played. He was a money player that always gave his best effort when the circumstances dictated. For this reason he was a winner wherever he played."

— *George Yardley, Hall of Famer (Ft. Wayne)*

"Jim was the first front court man who, in addition to being able to jump and rebound as well as any of today's players, could handle the ball as well as any back court man who ever played."

— *Paul Arizin, Hall of Famer (Philadelphia)*

"Even though he was a fierce competitor, Jim was known around the league as "Gentleman Jim." He was a true gentleman on and off the court. He was someone we always admired and considered our true friend."

— *Grady Lewis, Charter Board Member of Hall of Fame*

"Jim was good at every aspect of the game; running, shooting, passing, defense; he was a great all-around player and I loved him."

— *Slater "Dugie" Martin, Hall of Famer (Lakers)*

"The sporting community remembers him for his greatness on the court, and there is no question that he was one of the best players of all time, the Jordan of his era."

— *Todd Caso, Producer, NBA Entertainment*

"Jim Pollard of the old Minneapolis Lakers was one of the greatest basketball players ever to play in the NBA."

— *Sid Hartman, Minneapolis Star Tribune and WCCO Radio*

Jim Pollard
The Kangaroo Kid

Dolph Grundman

Nodin Press

Copyright © 2009 Adolph H. Grundman, all rights reserved. No part of this book may be reproduced in any form without the written consent of Nodin Press except for review purposes.

ISBN: 978-1-932472-86-8

Library of Congress No: 2009933511

Book design: John Toren

Nodin Press, LLC
530 N. Third Street,
Suite 120
Minneapolis, MN
55401

*To the Pollard family:
Arilee, Jeanne, Jack, and Jeff*

Acknowledgements

A mumber of people made it possible for me to collect the information necessary to write this biography of Jim Pollard. Jim's wife, Arilee Pollard, gave me access to all her scrapbooks, letters, and photographs related to Pollard's career. I was also able to interview a number of Lakers including Coach John Kundla and teammates Slater Martin, Jim Holstein, Lew Hitch, Bob Harrison, Vern Mikkelsen, Howie Schultz, Whitey Skoog, and Don Forman. Also helpful were interviews with players who played against Jim Pollard. They were Vince Boryla and Dick McGuire of the New York Knicks and Bill Calhoun, Arnie Risen, and Bobby Wanzer of the Rochester Royals.

In preparing the manuscript Ronald Mendell, a basketball historian in Wichita, Kansas, graciously volunteered to read the manuscript and offered mumerous helpful comments. Jeanne Pollard, Jim Pollard's daughter, also read early drafts and provided useful observations.

Finally, Emilio De Grazia, Professor Emeritus at Winona State University, distinguished author, and longtime friend provided editorial advice and encouragement.

Professional development grants from Metropolitan State College of Denver made it possible for me to take two productive research trips. The interlibrary loan department at the Auraria Library made possible to read the sports pages of Minneapolis, Syracuse, and Rochester newspapers. Finally, I want to offer a special thank you to Mrs. Sharon Roehling who typed the entire manuscript.

– Dolph Grundman
Department of History
Metropolitan State College of Denver

Table of Contents

1 The Natural 13

2 The War Years and AAU Basketball 28

3 "Mr. Pollard, Meet Mr. Mikan" 41

4 The Lakers Tackle the NBA 76

5 The String is Broken 89

6 The Lakers' Threepeat 101

7 "The Transition Game" 141

Index 172

Pollard makes a move to the basket against Arnie Risen of the Rochester Royals.

Introduction

> *Throughout his Hall of Fame career, Pollard demonstrated why his talents could easily transfer to today's game. Jim was the first player to really play the game "above the rim," where much of modern basketball is played.*
>
> – George Mikan

"Could he have played today?"

The question inevitably arises when basketball enthusiasts begin discussing the careers of those athletes who played professionally during the sport's formative years, when both teams and leagues appeared and disappeared with startling frequency. Those who actually played the game during the 1940s and 1950s invariably put Jim Pollard on the short list of those who would have excelled on the court even today. Pollard's graceful, acrobatic style has inspired comparisons with Clyde Drexler, Scotty Pippin, and even Michael Jordan. At 6'5", Pollard could run the court, shoot, dribble and was blessed with springs in his legs that earned him the nickname The Kangaroo Kid. He played above the rim.

Yet for a variety of reasons, Pollard's place in basketball history has been relatively neglected. His playing career spanned from 1942 through 1955; he retired just as pro basketball was about to come into its own. Although he was the high scorer for Stanford's 1942 NCAA championship team, he missed the championship game with the flu. World War II was in full swing by that time, and Pollard played his next three years of basketball for the armed services. The following two years, Pollard starred for teams that played in leagues and tournaments governed by the Amateur Athletic Union (AAU).

In 1947, Pollard signed his first contract with the Minneapolis Lakers, where he would play his entire professional career. Although he was a frequent all-league selection and All-Star, Minneapolis was a small-market city. And although the Minneapolis Lakers won a number of NBA championships during Pollard's time there, the focal point of the team's dynasty was George Mikan, the National Basketball Association's (NBA) first dominant big man.

But Jim Pollard had a special talent. His grace on the court was unmatched, though his family, teammates, students and colleagues often came to see it as merely an extension of the quiet confidence, grace and charm he brought to every part of his life. The time has come to examine the life and career of this extraordinary athlete in greater detail. Jim Pollard's story is fascinating in itself, and it also opens another window into the exciting history of professional basketball's early years.

1
THE NATURAL

*"He could always be found shooting baskets,
no matter the weather conditions. He was
tall, skinny and alone."*

– childhood friend Robert "Bobby" Moore

By the time Jim Pollard was born on July 9, 1922, in Oakland, California, his father, Henry Augustus "Gus" Pollard, had left his family. Jim had two sisters, Esther and Ruth, and a brother, Tom, but his siblings were much older than Jim. The youngest, Ruth, was already seventeen. Jim essentially grew up as an only child. His mother, Susan, made a living by managing an apartment building and taking in laundry. She was a faithful member of the Salvation Army, as was her estranged husband. As a boy Jim spent his time playing basketball and baseball at nearby parks, attending Salvation Army activities, or playing trumpet in the Salvation Army band.

Gus and Susie Pollard on their wedding day.

Gene Rock, who attended school with Jim from fourth

through the ninth grade, recalled that by fourth grade "he was already a head taller than the others." By the end of junior high, Jim's unusual athletic ability had become obvious. According to Rock, Pollard was quite popular among his fellow students, though he accepted his unusual talents without fanfare. When he was in ninth grade the students of Woodrow Wilson Junior High School elected Jim president of the Boys League, which presided over school programs.

During the mid-1930s a young Jim Pollard could be found playing basketball at Garfield Elementary School or Mosswood Park. The elementary school was close enough to the family's apartment that Jim's mother could blow a whistle to signal him that it was time to come home, but Mosswood Park was where Oakland's serious teenage basketball players tested their skills in games of three-on-three. Since there was little work for kids during the Depression, the park was always crowded, and the competition grew stiffer in the summer when the college players returned home.

Jim learned some important lessons at Mosswood Park. On one occasion he challenged a college player to a game of horse for a Coke. To his surprise, Jim lost, and when he admitted that he didn't have the money to pay his debt, his adversary punched him in the nose. The blow left Jim with a ridge on his nose that became a permanent part of his profile. But the bloody nose also taught him to keep his ego in check, to take nothing for granted, and to respect his opponents.

Another Mosswood encounter involved Leo McCaffrey, who would later become Jim's teammate at Stanford. Leo was not from the neighborhood, but he and two friends ventured over to Mosswood because they had heard it was the place to play "real basketball." In the middle of the game McCaffrey and his friends were playing, one of the players on the opposing team sprained an ankle. As McCaffrey later

Jim (left) with high school coach Al Kyte and Bobbie Moore

recalled, the player was replaced by a "tall, lanky person who had been watching from the sidelines." It was Jim Pollard, whose "speed, agility, timing, leaping ability...set him apart and took the game out of our hands." When the game was over, McCaffrey recalled, Jim "turned to us and with grace and a genuine smile said 'nice game'."

Ray Koehler also remembered playing basketball with Pollard in Oakland. Jim would arrive at his door every Saturday morning, and, as Koehler put it, "He would drag me down to Mosswood Park." Though there were players from both college and high school, and competition was fierce, Koehler recalled that "everyone watched Jim. He did things that were real hard to do look easy."

In 1938 Jim entered Oakland Technical High School. Al Kyte, a graduate of the University of California, Berkeley, was the basketball and baseball coach there, and he began to provide the male mentorship that had long been absent in Jim's life. Kyte was an old-fashioned disciplinarian. Like many coaches of his era, he opposed the use of a one-handed shot, which he considered mere showing off. At the time Jim's hero was Hank Luisetti, the great Stanford star who was revolutionizing the game with that shot. In one game Pollard had a chance to break a scoring record but Kyte yanked him after he took the forbidden shot. The young Pollard was contrite, and from that point on he deferred to the coach's authority.

Jim later told this story to his daughter, the lesson evidently being that no matter how good you thought you were, the coach's rules still applied to you. But the incident might also serve as an illustration of the fact that in the history of basketball, innovations often came from the players rather than the coaches.

At the time the coach's primary responsibility was to identify talent and guide it. But if a player found a new way of putting the ball in the basket or a new way of dribbling around his defender, the best coaches embraced the innovation. Because of his athletic ability, Pollard would be an innovator. He would do things on a basketball court that less talented players (and coaches) would never have dreamed of doing. In college, Pollard would return the one-handed jump shot to his offensive arsenal. What Al Kyte provided Jim Pollard as a coach at Oakland Technical High School was structure and love—even tough love. Jim respected this, and he and Al Kyte remained life-long friends.

During the basketball season Jim practiced endlessly. After high school basketball practice, teammate Bobby Moore recalled that "we would go home, eat, and come back to the gym and practice with teams who played in the Industrial League until 10 p.m." In Jim's three years at Tech, the Bulldogs racked up three Oakland Athletic League (OAL) basketball championships. In 1938 and 1939 Pollard won all-city and all-county team honors. In his senior year Jim scored 131 points in seven league games, a new OAL record. Ray Schwartz of the *Oakland Post Enquirer* wrote

THE NATURAL

TECH'S JIM "BIG

Jim "Big Spook" Pollard popular Tech Hi student and twice all-Alameda County center

Sixteen-year-old Jim "Big Spook" Pollard is six feet four inches tall, weighs 172 pounds, has brown eyes and sandy hair; and believe it or not girls, Jim claims he has no girl friend.

Pollard, a low senior at Oakland Technical High School, is very popular among the students; recently he refused a nomination for student body president. Both this refusal and the fact that he has no girl friend can probably be blamed to his extreme bashfulness.

For the past three years the "Big Spook" has played varsity basketball for Tech Hi. During the last O. A. L. season Jim surpassed the total point record for a season by 39 points, and twice he broke the total point record for a single game.

Through his outstanding playing he led his team to two championships and brought fame and fortune to himself; the fortune in the form of scholarship

Sitting on the lawn, during Tech's lunch period, are seen many of Pollard's friends and classmates

Pollard's mother, pictured above, is proud of her son and enjoys cooking Jim's favorite dish—macaroni

Lunch period is usually spent strolling the Tech campus. Above: Bob Moore, Ken Shields, and Joe Corroda are pictured with Pollard

This picture doesn't seem to coincide with Pollard's statement of having no girl friends. With Jim is Buzz White, Oakland's ace hurler

Jim recieved a lot of coverage in the Oakland Technical High School student newspaper.

17

that Pollard was "the *Greatest* prep player ever developed in Eastbay High School circles." At a time when team scores were in the 30s, Pollard averaged 18 points a game and occasionally scored as many as 29.

Pollard's teammate Bobby Moore also made the OAL's all-city and all-county team in 1939, during their senior year. He recalled "college scouts following us everywhere. Jim was unreal. He was the class of Northern California."

At the time Pollard was 6'4" and a lean 172 pounds. Ray Schwartz wrote that Jim "plucked the ball off the back board numerous times in order to stop opponents from attempting follow-up shots." On out of bounds plays underneath the basket, Moore would simply lob the ball "over the basket [and] Jim would outleap everyone and toss it in the basket." Before every game of their senior year, Moore said that their mothers "would give each of us a dollar and we would go to a small café near school and have a steak with the idea it was building up our energy." But the Depression was in full swing at the time and Jim's mother was barely making ends meet. Considered in retrospect, Moore doubted whether either of their parents could really afford that dollar.

According to Jeanne Pollard, Jim's daughter, in high school Jim had to get by on two pairs of pants. The student paper reported that "Jim claims he has no girl friend" and refused a nomination for student body president, due to "his extreme bashfulness." While this explanation rings true, the author may have failed to appreciate that Jim simply did not have the money to engage in "normal" teenage social life.

Jim attended his last semester at Oakland Tech in the fall of 1939. Because basketball was a two-semester sport, the bylaws of the Oakland Athletic League stipulated that midyear graduates could not compete, so Jim played that fall with

Golden State Creamery, one of the premier local amateur teams operating under the auspices of the Amateur Athletic Union (AAU).

For the first half of the twentieth century many basketball players who hoped to compete beyond their college years, especially if they lived west of the Mississippi River, played in leagues governed by the AAU. (There were professional teams in the Midwest and Atlantic States but salaries were too low to attract players outside these regions.) The best AAU teams were sponsored by large companies such as the Phillips Petroleum Company, though smaller businesses such as Golden State Creamery or the Buchan Bakery in Seattle also sponsored teams. The theory behind the league's amateur designation was that the players worked for the company and played basketball for fun. They were not being paid to play basketball *per se*. For example, some of the players for Golden State Creamery drove milk trucks. Jim Pollard's job, according to Ray Koehler, was to clean up the trucks. As a bonus, Jim got a couple of quarts of ice cream.

Though these teams were technically "amateur," the reality was complicated by the fact that businesses sponsoring them used them as marketing tools and the players themselves took the games very seriously. For them the ultimate goal was to play for the AAU national championship, held in Kansas City from 1921 to 1934 and in Denver from 1934 to 1968.

Pollard's team has an interesting history. It was a mix of Californians and AAU veterans who had played on such AAU powers as the Wichita Henrys, McPherson Globe Refiners, and Kansas City Healeys. In 1937 John Callahan, Ross McBurney, and Melvin Miller joined Golden State Creamery. They had been fixtures on the Wichita Henrys, a team that had won three consecutive national championships

Members of the Golden State Creamery head to Denver for the AAU finals. L to R Top to Bottom: Mel Miller, Al Nelson, Bill Wheately, Kenny Meitz, Manager Orrie (Skipper) Anwyl shaking hands with Pollard, Johnny Callahan, Clarence Anderson, Bob Weir and Ralph Hillsman.

between 1930 and 1932. In 1938, this trio was joined by Bill Wheatley, a 1936 AAU All-American with the McPherson Globe Refiners and captain of the 1936 gold medal U.S. Olympic basketball team. The last of the Kansas contingent to join Golden State Creamery was Bob Weir, a 6'6" center who played on Kansas City's 1935 and 1938 AAU championship teams.

The Californians on the team included St. Mary's Clarence "Swede" Anderson and Ken Meitz. In 1939 these two played with San Francisco's Olympic Club, a third place finisher in the national tournament. Bob Duffy and Ralph Hillsman had played at Cal. By 1940, Callahan was the coach and McBurney had retired.

During his time on the Golden State Creamery team

Pollard (whom these AAU veterans called The Kid) had the opportunity to test his skills against far tougher competition than he had met up with in high school, and in the process he also picked up more than a few new tricks. And because the teams were technically amateur, Jim would not forfeit the opportunity to play in college.

At the end of the regular league season, Golden State won the *Oakland Tribune* Industrial Athletic Association Tournament. The victory brought with it $1000 to pay for the expenses to take the team to Denver for the AAU National Basketball Championship of America. It was Golden State's fourth consecutive trip to Denver. Its best finish had been in 1937 when it lost in the quarterfinals. The team had been put together with the idea that the veterans would get one more crack at the national title. Wheatley, Weir, and Miller announced that this would be their last tournament. Pollard was still deciding where he would attend college. Although he had no way of knowing, this would be the first of four trips to Denver for the 17-year-old phenomena.

From the late 1930s to the early 1960s the AAU tournament was one of the biggest sporting events in Denver. In the 1940 tournament Golden State was one of the four top-seeded teams among fifty that attended. The tournament was played on the stage of the Denver Auditorium, a venue normally used for musical events. Beginning on Sunday the teams would battle for the right to play on the following Saturday for the championship. Harry Farrar, a sports columnist for *The Denver Post*, once described the tournament as "a combination of state fair, southern social, and fish fry." Fans would often stay for most of the day and on into the evening, hoping to see an upset, a favorite player, or a new star. Denver had rabid fans and the 1940 tournament was keenly anticipated because the local team, the Nuggets, had won two of the three previous championships. Denver's stars, Jack McCracken, a skilled guard with ice in his veins, and Robert "Ace" Gruenig, a 6'8" center with a deadly sweeping hook shot, were already basketball legends in the West.

In its first game, Golden State edged Mobile Oilers of Denver 47-41. Weir was high scorer for the Creamers with 14 and Pollard followed with 9. A 49-40 victory over the University Avenue Coalers of Des Moines, Iowa, put Golden State in the quarter finals. In the quarterfinals Golden State dominated the St. Louis Rangers 37-19. The writer covering the game described the Creamers as "big and rough with scorers." He was particularly impressed with how Pollard, Wheatley, Weir and Meitz ran the fast-break against the Rangers.

The victory set up a semifinal match with the Denver Nuggets, who dominated Golden State 46-32 before a capacity crowd of six thousand screaming fans. In the finals, the Phillips 66ers nipped Denver 39-36. Golden State beat S.L. Savidge of Seattle in the consolation game 50-36—its best performance in tournament history.

For Jim Pollard the tournament must have been a confidence builder. Before the tournament, Mel Miller, a two-time AAU All-America, told Art Geen of the *Oakland Tribune* that Jim "is gonna become one of the greatest players in history," and Jim's performance in Denver did nothing to lower Miller's estimation of the Kid's potential.

With the tournament behind him, Jim began to consider seriously where he would attend college. Initially, the University of Southern California had the inside track, especially since Gene Rock, Jim's boyhood friend, played for the Trojans. But Stanford pursued Jim relentlessly. Bobby Moore remembered a recruiting visit to the home of a judge in the Piedmont area of Oakland. Bobby's father let him use the family's 1931 Model A convertible to drive to a house surrounded by Lincolns, Cadillacs, and Mercedes. The butler let them in, and Bobby and Jim were greeted by the Stanford basketball team and its great All-American, Hank Luisetti. It was a memorable evening for two working class kids from Oakland. But it was Everett Dean, Stanford's basketball coach, who won the bidding war for Pollard. Dean simply convinced Jim's mother that he was the best person to guide Jim's development as a basketball player and as a person.

Everett S. Dean was one of the great gentlemen of college basketball. Born on a farm in Livonia, Indiana, he won All-America honors in basketball at the University of Indiana. He was also a star on the baseball team. After graduating in 1922, Dean coached for three years at Carlton College in Northfield, Minnesota. He then returned to Indiana where he coached baseball and basketball. His Hoosier basketball teams won three Big Ten titles and compiled a 162-93 record.

In the fall of 1938, Dean replaced John Bunn as the coach of Stanford's basketball team. The Indians had just completed an unforgettable run, winning three Pacific Coast titles in a row. In the process their star forward, Hank Luisetti, broke all of Stanford's scoring records. While Dean did not have the pleasure of coaching Luisetti, Stanford's recent success made his recruiting easier. At a time when college programs relied on local players, Dean was also fortunate that San Francisco and Oakland were rich in basketball talent. Under coach Benny Neff's leadership, Lowell High School in San Francisco turned out one college player after another between 1930 and 1960. Three of his players—Don Burness, Bill Cowden, and Howie Dallmar—started for Stanford in 1941-42, along with Oakland players Ed Voss and Pollard himself. Oakland schools also gave Stanford Leo McCaffrey,

Don Williams, Kenny Davidson, and the team's sixth man that year, Jack Dana.

Stanford's starting five averaged 6'4" in 1941, which earned them the nickname The Tall Redwoods of California. The starters were also fast and strong. Because of the Luisetti influence, they all shot one-handed. Coach Dean, according to Bill Cowden, "wanted us to shoot with our feet on the ground but once he saw Pollard, Burness, and Dallmar shoot while jumping, he revised his thinking." Dean liked his team to play multiple defenses and used set plays on offense. Pollard thought "our starting five or six could guard anybody."

When Jim entered Stanford in the fall of 1940, freshmen were not eligible to play varsity basketball. In 1941, he was the freshmen team's high scorer. By his sophomore year, according to Stanford's program, Jim was 6'4½" and weighed 185 pounds. In the 1941-42 regular season Stanford was 22-3 overall and 11-1 in the Southern Division of the Pacific Coast Conference.

At this time an invitation to the National Collegiate Athletic Association (NCAA) basketball tournament depended on beating the winner of the conference's Northern Division. In mid-March Stanford squared off against Oregon State at the Stanford Pavilion in a best-of-three series. The Californians won the first and third games to earn a trip to the NCAA tournament, with Pollard the leading scorer in both victories.

In 1942 the NCAA basketball tournament was in its infancy. The University of Oregon had won the first NCAA basketball championship in 1939. There was no Final Four. Instead, the nation was divided into Eastern and Western Regions. The winner of each region then met for the national championship. In 1942 a mere eight teams were invited to the tournament.

Co-Captain & guard Bill Cowden, guard Howie Dallmar, center Ed Voss, forward Jim Pollard, Co-Captain & forward Don Burness, Coach Everett Dean.

After defeating Oregon State, the Stanford team got up bright and early the following morning to catch an 8 a.m. train for Kansas City where it would play Rice Institute. (The budget was not rich enough for air travel.) In recalling the experience, Fred Linari said, "It was kind of low-key. We were focused on winning, but given the dynamics of the time with no TV or media hype, we didn't think it was a big deal." And Pollard remarked, "Heck, I don't even remember a newspaper guy from San Francisco or Oakland being there."

Stanford's co-caption, Don Burness, was out with a badly sprained ankle, but Pollard took up the slack, scoring 26 to lead Stanford to a 53-43 victory over Rice. The next night the Californians beat the University of Colorado 46-35 to win the Western Regional, and one writer observed that Pollard, who led all scorers with 17 points, "worked so smoothly he looked as if he were floating."

Dartmouth College won the Eastern Regional in New Orleans to set up the championship game at Kansas City. Its coach, Ozzie Cowles, had played for Everett Dean at Carlton College. Stanford remained in Kansas City for the week as it prepared for the contest. As luck would have it, Pollard caught the flu and was too weak to play in the championship game. Despite the losses of Burness and Pollard, Stanford got hot in the second half of the championship game and ran away from Dartmouth 53-38. Howie Dallmar led all players with 15 points, while Jack Dana, normally the sixth man, added 14.

Despite missing the championship game, Pollard was the tournament's leading scorer. The tournament grossed $23,500 and netted $1500 after expenses. Stanford's share of the pot was $193.75. The players received gold basketball charms and the team was presented with a gold-plated trophy described by one observer as "bigger than the Sir Thomas Lipton Yachting Cup."

The tournament was held against the background of World War II. After the season Pollard enlisted in the United State Coast Guard and never played another college game. But his two years at Stanford had made a lasting impact on Jim. He remained friends with Everett Dean for the rest of his life, often seeking his advice. Much later Pollard said of Dean: "He's one of the nicest guys I ever met." Dean, in turn, remembered Pollard as "a very natural basketball player. He had a basketball sense, know how. He was just born with it. He could pass, and he was one of the first men to use the jump shot. He also had great speed." Jim's teammates agreed. Fred Linari thought Pollard was "the Michael Jordan of his day." Leo McCaffrey thought Jim was "the best player around."

While his friends, teammates, and sportswriters were united in their praise of Jim's skills, they also liked him as a person. Ray Koehler recalled that during pick-up games at Mosswood Park Jim would insist that other teammates shoot the ball, rather than leaving it up to him to score. Koehler had a special affection for Jim because Jim had helped him through a difficult period of his teenage years when his parents separated and he was forced to live with a local teacher. Lacking the guidance of a parent, Koehler felt that Jim and another friend had kept him on the good side of the tracks.

Art Geen, who covered Jim as a sportswriter for the *Oakland Tribune*, wrote: "Pollard's the type of lad who'll sacrifice his own scoring, and shots, for the ball club—will hold back, in fact, to pass off to others, and would rather play a good floor-game than tank a fist full of points."

But though Jim was thoughtful, modest, and unselfish, he was also an indifferent student. His friend Fred Linari recalled that he was simply not interested in studying, preferring to participate in recreational league play. It was an unending struggle for him to maintain his eligibility.

Outside of basketball and baseball Jim loved music. He and Fred Linari would sing duets on the team bus going to San Francisco or Berkeley "We must have been pretty good," Linari later recalled, "no one moved or yelled 'quiet.'" At one of the reunions for the 1942 team, Pollard confessed that he had been part of a group that had sneaked out of their hotel in Los Angeles to listen to Tommy Dorsey and Frank Sinatra perform at the Palladium, returning well after curfew. "It was no big deal," Jim chuckled, "I think I ended up having two cokes."

2

THE WAR YEARS AND AAU BASKETBALL

Pollard is listed as a center ... but he is really center, guard, and forward bundled into one sleek greyhound of a frame.

– Chet Nelson, *Rocky Mountain News*

During the war many of America's best college basketball players were drafted or enlisted in the armed services, and many of them played for squads organized by the various service branches. Some colleges cancelled their schedules during the war years; Stanford did not compete in basketball between 1943 and 1945.

In the summer of 1942, Pollard was working in the shipyards in Alameda. One day after work he got involved in a pick-up game against the Coast Guard team that was stationed nearby. After the game, the team's coach, Verdie Cox, approached Jim and invited him to play with the CG—they'd "pick him up." Jim was actually too tall to be in the Coast Guard, but during the enlistment process he scrunched down enough to meet the legal height requirement.

Pollard began playing with Coast Guard's Alameda Sea Lions in the fall of 1942 and soon became a star. Most of his teammates were from San Francisco or Oakland. Hal Wood had played at St. Mary's, Mel Dropo at San Francisco Junior College, and Joe O'Malley at the University of San Francisco. One of the highlights of this season was a match up on January 9, 1943, between the Sea Lions and St. Mary's Pre-Flight five starring Hank Luisetti.

Following his stellar career at Stanford, in 1941 Luisetti had led San Francisco's Olympic Club to a second place finish in the National AAU tournament in Denver. The next year Luisetti played with the Phillips 66ers out of Bartlesville, Oklahoma, which lost to Denver in the AAU finals. In both years he was an AAU All-American and a favorite of the Denver fans and media. Luisetti was six years older than Pollard, and the press sometimes referred to Pollard as a "second Luisetti."

The match-up between the Sea Lions and St. Mary's was a nail-biter, but with four minutes to go and the score tied 31-31, the Pre-Flight five outscored the Sea Lions 14-5 to win 45-36. Six thousand fans at the Civic Auditorium watched Pollard edge Luisetti for the scoring honors 22 to 20.

In February the Sea Lions entered the Pacific Association AAU tournament, a favorite of Bay Area basketball fans. The winner of the tournament earned an all-expenses paid trip to the National AAU Tournament in Denver. Bob Feerick, Fred Scolari, Chuck Hanger, Ed Conroy, Morris "Mushy" Silver, and Paul Napolitano were just a few of the notable players in the tournament Bay Area that the fans had been following for years, from high school to college and on to local AAU teams. The Sea Lions won four straight, including a 45-29 victory over the University of San Francisco in the finals, to win the tournament. Pollard was the tournament's high scorer and poured in 23 in the title game. On defense Pollard took advantage of rules that allowed goal tending, and according to the local papers, he jumped "to fantastic heights to slap away everything USF unloaded."

The Seal Lions, accompanied by the Coast Guard band, arrived in Denver riding an eighteen-game winning streak, but they were eliminated in their first game by the Naval Air Station from Norman, Oklahoma. Pollard himself had a spectacular game, which Chet Nelson of the *Rocky Mountain News* described as "one of the greatest individual performances seen here in many years. He poured in 24 points, cleared rebounds and flipped fancy passes like a shortstop throwing to first base." In the last minute of regulation play Pollard scored three baskets—one of them a desperation shot just before the final gun to drive the game into overtime. But the Sea Lions were shut out 3-0 in the overtime period.

The nail-biting game thrilled the 4,500 fans who watched it, and so did the Coast Guard band. Jack Carberry, veteran sports columnist for *The Denver Post*, thought that it "gave out with the grandest jam, jive, and boogie woogie session to be heard in this man's town since bands started playing music."

In 1943 basketball promoters in the Bay Area created the Northern Basketball Association. Ten service teams were involved along with the San Francisco Athletic Club. Since both the Alameda Coast Guard and St. Mary's Pre-Flight were in the league, a renewal of the Pollard-Luisetti rivalry was guaranteed.

As the Sea Lions prepared for the season, they strengthened their roster by adding local standouts Paul Napolitano, Kevin O'Shea, Al Conti and Ernie Filiberti. On January 15, 1944, eleven thousand fans jammed San Francisco's Civic Auditorium to watch St. Mary's Air Devils edge the Coast Guard 35 to 34. This time Luisetti topped Pollard for scoring honors. Twelve days later, Jim scored 17 against Abe Saperstein's Harlem Globetrotters who edged the Coast Guard 43-40. On February 26, before a sold out crowd at the Civic Auditorium, Luisetti scored 32 as the Air Devils topped the Sea Lions 48-43. George Ziegenfuss, who starred at the University of Washington, limited Pollard to nine points. The St. Mary's five added Howie Dallmar, Pollard's Stanford teammate, for this game and the rest of the season. In March the two teams met one last time in the finals of the the *Examiner-Pacific* tournament. In another close game St. Mary's Pre-Flight prevailed 41-38 as Luisetti scored 19, while Ziegenfuss once again held Pollard to nine points.

That tournament brought to an end a remarkable season in the Bay Area. In the midst of the uncertainties of war, fans had enjoyed watching two of the region's most talented players tangle time and again, and arguments continued for decades among basketball junkies as to the relative merits of these two great future Hall of Fame players.

At about this time Jim began to get serious about a young woman named Arilee Hansen. Although they never dated in high school, Jim had invited her to a football game during his time at Stanford. The courtship became more serious when he was stationed at the Alameda Coast Guard Training Station. Arilee attended San Jose State for her first three years of college, but transferred to San Francisco State for her senior year so that she could live at home and be more available for her new suitor, and, as she later recalled, Jim started "hanging around the house."

While Jim was shy and cautious, Arilee was outgoing and a born organizer. When Jim was playing baseball and basketball at Oakland Tech, Arilee was president of the Girls Athletic Association. Her father, William, a high school chemistry and physics teacher, and her mother, Banna Alma, an elementary school teacher, were graduates of the University of California. Because her father was an amateur geologist, Arilee and her sister and three brothers made yearly trips to America's national parks. Yosemite was a favorite.

Jim and Arilee in front of Arilee's family home.

Before long Jim and Arilee were engaged. And Jim presented her with the engagement ring in a typically playful way. As Jim's daughter Jeanne tells the story:

> *Dad had a sense of humor, a pretty wry one at that. February 13 was Mom's birthday. Dad was playing with the Coast Guard Sea Lions at Kezar Stadium in San Francisco, and invited Mom to come. Before the game began, he gave her a box to hold, and said he'd make some baskets for her. He made 13 in the first half, and 13 in the second for 26 points. Later, he took the box and gave her the engagement ring, asking her to marry him. She sure was pleased!*

Unfortunately, several weeks before the wedding, Jim's mother died. The two had been very close and her death left Jim with a profound sense of loss, but after much discussion, Jim and Arilee decided against postponing their wedding, and on June 24, 1944, they were married at Emmanuel Presbyterian Church in Oakland. Shortly after the wedding, in the fall of 1944, the U.S. Coast Guard transferred Pollard to Honolulu. The couple would not be reunited until after the war.

In Honolulu Jim played for the U.S. Coast Guard Cutters

in the Central Pacific Area league (CPA). He was the league's high scorer and was chosen for the all-CPA team. Gayle Hayes of the *Honolulu Advertisers* described him as "the 'perfect player' of the league." He led the Cutters to the championship in the Schofield Barracks Invitational Tournament and was named the tournament's outstanding player.

Following the bombing of Hiroshima and Nagasaki, Japan surrendered to the United States and hostilities came to an end. For Americans in uniform, this meant pursing dreams put on hold because of the war. Jim Pollard had to decide on how best to capitalize on his basketball talents. In September, 1945, Harry Roos of the Chicago American Gears said he was prepared to "make an excellent offer" if Pollard wanted to play professional basketball, and Bill Mortola of the Dardi Company in San Francisco, was prepared to offer "any reasonable deal you may want" to play for the company's AAU team. But Jim still had a service obligation with the Coast Guard, and when they transferred him to San Diego, he decided to sign with the San Diego Dons in the American Basketball League (ABL).

The Dons were sponsored by William T. Rice, a San Diego dentist and basketball enthusiast. The Dons coach, Tee Connelley, was a veteran of almost ten years of AAU basketball. Connelley had played on one of Denver's championship teams and then moved to San Francisco where he played on several AAU teams. Joining Pollard and Connelley were Tom McCarty of the University San Francisco, Alva "Allie" Paine, an All-American at the University of Oklahoma, and Fon Johnson, an AAU veteran.

Since the ABL was governed by AAU rules, Pollard retained the option of returning to college. In fact, Eddie Griffith, sports editor of the *San Diego Journal*, reported that

Jim planned to return to Stanford where he had two years of eligibility. The ABL included Phillips 66, the dominant amateur team of the 1940s; Denver, the 66ers arch rival; Kansas City, which had sponsored AAU teams for over two decades; Salt Lake City, another AAU hot spot; and four teams from California. Some of the ABL's big name players besides Pollard, were Fred Scolari, Alex Hannum, Arnie Ferrin, Jim "Scat" McNatt, Robert "Ace" Gruenig, Jesse "Cab" Renick, Gordon "Shorty" Carpenter, Andy Duncan, and Frank Lubin.

In his first year Pollard was the ABL's leading scorer. Chet Nelson of the *Rocky Mountain News* wrote that there was a consensus among players and fans that Pollard was the best player in the league. Along with his many skills, Nelson wrote, that Jim "isn't one to hog the limelight and forget team play in his own behalf."

In March 1946 sixty-four teams met in Denver to compete for the National AAU championship. The tournament was loaded with talent. Service teams brought future professional stars like Bobby Wanzer, Alex Groza, and Andy Phillip. The Dons strengthened their roster for the tournament by adding Kenny Sailors, the leader of Wyoming's 1943 NCAA championship team. After winning three games, the Dons reached the semifinals, but would have to play without Sailors, who flew to New York to play in the East-West college game at Madison Square Garden.

Despite the loss of Sailors, the Dons edged Denver 46-42 in a game that, according to Leonard Cahn of the *Rocky Mountain News* featured "one of the most brilliant duels in tournament history." When Jim outscored Denver's "Ace" Gruenig, 20 to 18, he won Cahn's respect. The Denver writer reported that this was Pollard's "third straight 40-minute game." Cahn thought "if ever a player was deserving of participating in the championship game, that man is Pollard."

Ray McGovern of *The Denver Post* agreed. "Gruenig never played harder against the new wonder man," he wrote, but "the spring in the legs and the air in the lungs of the younger Pollard were factors the Acer could not cope with."

In 1946 the Dons were the Cinderella team, but the fairy tale ended in the championship game when the Californians lost to the Philips 66ers 45-34. The game was tied at halftime, but Phillips had too much depth for the Dons. The 66ers rotated four defenders on Pollard who finished the game with 10 points. Two members of the 1948 gold medal Olympic team, Gordon "Shorty" Carpenter (15) and Jesse "Cab" Renick (9), led Phillips in scoring.

For Pollard, the championship game was the end of a spectacular week and season. He was the tournament's leading scorer and was named to the AAU All America team. Perhaps Chet Nelson of the *Rocky Mountain News* best captured his blend of skills when he wrote: "Pollard is listed as a center… but he is really a center, guard and forward bundled into one sleek, greyhound type of frame." At the end of March the Helms Athletic Foundation named Pollard the "Southern California Athlete of the Month for February 1946."

As Jim Pollard prepared to leave the Coast Guard in 1946, there was a great deal of speculation about where he would play the following year. Twentieth Century-Fox, an AAU team, the Rochester Royals of the National Basketball League (NBL), and the Philadelphia Warriors of the newly formed Basketball Association of America (BAA) were among the teams courting him. Foremost in Pollard's mind, however, was that he wanted to be in a position to finish his degree. "Ever since I was seven years old in Oakland, California," he wrote, "I have had one big ambition in life. That is to be a successful and well-thought of basketball coach. To achieve this ambition it is necessary to have a college degree."

Les Harrison tried to convince Jim that he could finish his degree at the University of Rochester while playing for the Royals. The Royals would also help Arilee find a teaching position. Pollard must have also been concerned about the style of play in the NBL, because Harrison tried to reassure Jim that the NBL was "fast and crowd pleasing. It isn't anything like that old game of tug of war which the pros played years ago."

But Pollard turned Harrison down, preferring to remain closer to home. He signed with the Oakland Bittners, a new team in the American Basketball League. Sponsored by Lou Bittner, a successful Oakland businessman, the Bittner roster featured a collection of Bay Area standouts, including Paul Napolitano, Don Williams, Bob Alameida, and Warren "Slats" Taulbee. Don Burness, Jim's teammate a Stanford, and Bill Calhoun were also on the team. The coach, Bill Wheatley, had been a teammate of Jim's on Golden State Creamery. During the season Pollard attended San Francisco State and most likely made only token appearances at the Bittners offices. The checks were written to Arilee Pollard.

In choosing to return to Oakland, Pollard may have been persuaded that the ABL was about to become a professional league. In the fall of 1946, Harry Hannin, Director of the *Chicago Herald-American* College All-Star Basketball Game, thought so. In trying to recruit Pollard for the College All Star Basketball Classic, Hannin tried to persuade him that he would not lose his amateur status. Moreover, Hannin thought the issue was irrelevant since "it is a known fact that

The Bittners went to Hollywood with Jim in 1946 when he was being honored with the Helms Award. Here we see them with Peggy Ann Gardner. Jim is standing behind Peggy. Luisetti in standing at far right.

the league in which you are involved is only about a year away from becoming a professional league, because I, as well as you and everyone connected, knows that it is far from an amateur set-up." Pollard did not play in the 1946 College All-Star Classic and focused his attention on Oakland's season.

The Bittners did not taste defeat until January 5, 1947, when, after sixteen wins, it lost in Salt Lake City to the Deseretts 45-44. After the game Jim sent a telegram to Arilee: "We played terrible in the second half." Five weeks later eight thousand fans packed into the Oakland Auditorium and watched the Bittners trounce the powerful Phillips 66ers 59-47. Don Williams, who scored 13 for the Bittners, called it the most important game in Oakland's history. At the time the 66ers had won forty-three consecutive games and featured Bob Kurland, a seven-foot All-American center from Oklahoma A & M. After falling behind by ten points, the 66ers closed the gap to one point as Kurland stood under the basket and batted balls away from the basket. The Bittners adjusted by shooting higher arching shots and won by twelve. Pollard led all players with 19 and Bob Brachman of the *San Francisco Examiner* called him "the master court strategist." Bud Browning, coach of the 66ers, called Pollard "the greatest I have ever watched."

In a rematch in Bartlesville on February 26, the 66ers squeezed by the Bittners 36-32. Bob Kurland led all scorers with 18 and R. C. Pitts, a defensive specialist, limited Pollard to 4 points. Almost fifty years later Pitts told me that Jim Pollard was as good as any he had played against. Pitts was able to put the clamps on Pollard by lightly touching his shooting arm just enough to throw his shot off without being detected for a foul.

The Bittners finished the ABL in second place with an 18-2 record, a game behind Phillips.

In post-season play the Bittners won the ABL tournament by beating the Denver Nuggets 52-38. The coaches named Pollard to the all-tournament team and also the tourney's most valuable player. Just before the tournament R. C. Embry of the Baltimore Bullets met with Jim and offered him a $10,000 contract. Before making any decision on his future, however, Pollard decided to focus his attention one last time on capturing a national AAU championship.

The Bittners were not seriously challenged in the opening rounds of the tournament, and they overwhelmed Denver 55 to 40 in the semifinals. After watching the game Chet Nelson called Pollard "the roundball game's newest and probably greatest 'superman'." In describing his play Nelson said: "He batted field goals out of the air as easily as you could swat a fly. He was a leech on defense. He passed the ball around as though he owned it."

Pollard led all players that night with 27 points, but the

following night the Phillips 66ers clobbered Oakland 62-41 for its fifth consecutive title. The key to the 66ers victory, once again, was the dogged defense of R. C. Pitts, who limited Pollard to 5 points. For the second straight year Pollard was named to the AAU All-America team, but that individual honor was scant compensation for failing once again to win the title.

The end of the 1947 basketball season presented Jim Pollard with a dilemma. He was about to turn twenty-five and it was clear that Oakland was not going to field a professional basketball team. The only reason to play another year of AAU basketball was to remain eligible for the 1948 Olympics. Ever since he had played with Golden State Creamery, Jim had remained close to Bill Wheatley, a teammate in 1940 and his coach with the Bittners. Wheatley captained the 1936 Olympic basketball team and encouraged Jim to follow in his footsteps. The hitch was that the American Olympic Basketball Committee used a tournament to select the Olympic basketball players. In 1948 the plan was to invite the top three AAU teams from the national AAU tournament plus the college teams that had won national tournaments to New York City. The finalists of a tournament at Madison Square Garden would name five players and the Olympic Basketball Committee would name four at-large players from the tournament teams. Since there was no guarantee that the Bittners would finish in one of the three top spots at the National AAU Tournament, Pollard decided that his best option would be to take the best professional offer that was available to him.

3
"Mr. Pollard, Meet Mr. Mikan"

"It must be said emphatically that Pollard and Mikan are performing brilliantly."

- Joe Hendrickson, *Minneapolis Tribune*

In the spring of 1947, when Pollard made the decision to turn pro, two professional basketball leagues were struggling to capture the imagination, and the ticket-revenues, of the fans. The older league, the National Basketball League (NBL), dated back only to 1937. Its most stable franchises were the Rochester Royals, the Oshkosh All-Stars, the Sheboygan Redskins, and the Fort Wayne Zollner Pistons. Other teams joined the league, moved from city to city, or collapsed outright with disturbing frequency.

It was a volatile business, but that didn't stop a group of sports entrepreneurs from organizing a second league, the Basketball Association of America (BAA), in June of 1946. The teams in the BAA were owned by arenas such as the Boston Garden, Madison Square Garden, and the Chicago Stadium. Given the popularity of college basketball, the arena managers were convinced that a professional league made up of former college stars had a good chance of success. Professional basketball would also provide another event to keep the arenas, and their concession doors, open. The BAA owners also felt that they could do better than the NBL because their venues were in bigger markets.

The potential for success seemed great. In the BAA a franchise cost $1000 and a salary cap for a twelve-player roster was set at $55,000. BAA rules were slightly different from those used in the college game. A game lasted 48 minutes rather than 40, player disqualification came after 6 fouls rather than 5, and zone defenses were prohibited. The owners, who would call themselves the Board of Governors, named Maurice Podoloff president of the league. At the time, Podoloff was also president of the American Hockey League. He had a law degree from Yale and loads of business experience.

The appearance of a second professional league worked to the bargaining advantage of players like Pollard, and after the BAA's first year, Podoloff called a meeting of the two leagues to deal with the problem of bidding wars. As an example, Podoloff said, "Every team in either league has made a ridiculous offer to Jim Pollard, yet he continues to hold us off and then we go into another round of bidding. And still nobody has been able to sign him." In fact, before the meeting he had been signed by the Minneapolis Lakers for $12,000 a year plus a signing bonus of $1,000. The club agreed that any future contract would have to be at least $12,000. At about that time the Lakers also signed three of Pollard's Bittner teammates—Bill Durkee, John Rocker, and Paul Napolitano. In signing with the Lakers, Pollard was taking a chance. The team lacked a proven track record. Then again, there were no sure bets in the world of professional basketball.

Jim had recieved offers from St. Louis, Chicago, Baltimore, Philadelphia, Rochester, Indianapolis, and Oshkosh, but he was confident that Minneapolis would win the title in its first year of existence.

"I know what Paul Napolitano, Jack Rocker and Bill Durkee can do," he told one local reporter. "They were stars with our Oakland Bittners last year. With boys like Don Carlson, Tony Jaros and Sid Tanenbaum around, I can't see how we can fail to have one of the outstanding pro teams in the country."

While there is some disagreement on the details, the general outline of the Lakers' origins follow a familiar pattern. In every city there were sportswriters involved in the promotion of athletic events and teams. In Minneapolis one of those people was Sid Hartman. A street-smart kid who loved sports, Hartman became a sports reporter for the *Minneapolis Times* and then the *Tribune*. In 1947 Minneapolis had no major league teams. Hartman believed that pro basketball had a future and that Minneapolis could get in on the ground floor. He sold his idea to Morris Chalfen and Ben Berger, two local businessmen familiar with the entertainment business. Another ground-floor investor was Max Winter, a sometime fight promoter and owner of the 620

Jim with Ben Berger after signing with the Lakers.

Club, a popular restaurant "Where Turkey was King." As luck would have it, Morris Winston, the owner of the Detroit Gems, was desperately trying to sell his team after having finished last in the NBL the previous season. Hartman offered Winston $15,000 for the franchise and the Detroiter gladly accepted the offer.

Before long Ben Berger had bought out Winter and Hartman. Chalfen retained 25 percent of the club, but from the beginning preferred to stay in the background. Max Winter remained with the club as general manager.

Berger's was a rags-to-riches story. He was born Beryl Nachum Berger on March 5, 1897, in Ostrowiec, Poland. Born into a modest family, he experienced the sting of anti-Semitism which was severe in Poland. At the age of 16, Berger persuaded his father to allow him to go to America. He had had little formal schooling in Poland and received none in the United States. Bright and energetic, he changed his name to Ben and worked diligently to perfect his English and to make his way in the world.

Between 1913 and 1923 Berger lived primarily in Fargo, North Dakota, with a hitch in the U.S. Army during World War I. He became involved in a series of successful business ventures and eventually bought a string of movie theaters. This took him to Grand Forks, North Dakota, where he sold his theaters to Paramount in 1930. In the 1930s, Berger moved to Minneapolis and continued to invest in the theater business. Before owning the Lakers, he was probably best known as the owner of Shiek's Café, which became a favorite night club in the Twin Cities.

Berger knew absolutely nothing about basketball, but he knew a great deal about promoting entertainment. He approached professional basketball as a part of the entertainment industry. While ownership of the Lakers would produce joy and frustration, Berger thought, on balance, it enhanced his place in the community. He told Robert K. Krishef, his biographer, "It made me front-page news, a big shot around town. It was a door-opener for me—and because of that, other Jews got through the door, too—into Minneapolis service clubs." If sports helped to break down anti-Semitism, "that still made it plenty worthwhile."

After signing the four Californians, Sid Hartman persuaded Berger to invest $15,000 to purchase the contracts of two University of Minnesota stars, Tony Jaros and Don "Swede" Carlson. Jaros was from northeast Minneapolis, a neighborhood composed mainly of Eastern Europeans. At Edison High School Jaros starred in football, baseball, and basketball. He set city scoring records in basketball at Edison before moving on to the University of Minnesota, where he played baseball and basketball. As a sophomore Jaros finished second in the Big Ten basketball scoring race. At 6'3" and 215 pounds, he established a reputation as a no-nonsense blue collar player. In 1942 the war interrupted his athletic career and he saw duty in France. After the war Jaros returned to the University of Minnesota for his junior year. He then signed to play professional baseball with the Minneapolis Millers and professional basketball with the Chicago Stags.

Don Carlson was another Edison High product and the leader of its 1937 state championship team. At 6'1", Carlson played a forward position and was an All Conference selection at the University of Minnesota. He was voted the most valuable player for the Chicago Stags in 1946-47.

The Lakers added three more local stars when they signed Warren Ajax, Don Smith, and Ken Excel. The latter two had starred at Minneapolis's Roosevelt High School and all three played for Dave MacMillan at the University of Minnesota.

The Lakers management's first choice to coach the team was Joe Hutton, the basketball coach at Hamline College in St. Paul. Hutton had played for Everett Dean at Carlton College and had developed a small college powerhouse at Hamline. Howie Schultz, Joe Hutton, Jr., and Vern Mikkelsen (who went on to a Hall of Fame career with the Lakers) all played at Hamline. When Hutton declined the opportunity to coach the Lakers, Sid Hartman turned to John Kundla, who took the job. Kundla had his doubts about pro basketball's future in the Twin Cities, but Hartman offered him a three-year contract at $6,000 a year, twice what he was earning at St. Thomas College in St. Paul.

Like his players, Kundla had used athletics to make his way in the world. His parents, John and Anna Kundla, were immigrants from Czechoslovakia. John Kundla's father, like so many eastern European immigrants, found work in America's expanding industrial economy. When John Kundla was born on July 3, 1916, in Star Junction, Pennsylvania, his father was working for Jones and Lauglin Steel in Aliquippa, Pennsylvania.

When John was five his mother left her husband and took John to Minneapolis. She had family in northeast Minneapolis and found work as a cook at Dayton's Department Store. Until he started elementary school, Slovakian rather than English was spoken in the Kundla home. John learned English in Emerson Elementary School and helped to teach his mother; she eventually became an American citizen. In eighth grade Richard Kempter, the physical education teacher, introduced Kundla to the fundamentals of basketball. In tenth grade, he and his mother moved to south Minneapolis where he attended Central High School. Kundla remembered Wes Mitchell, Central's basketball coach, as a good mentor.

In his junior year John experienced a big growth spurt and started on the varsity in his junior and senior years. In 1933, when Kundla graduated from Central High, his mother married Ellis Matson and the couple moved to Washington. John remained in Minneapolis where he worked at the Field's Hotel for room and board. He earned his spending money by working the desk at the YMCA. John continued to develop his basketball skills by playing AAU ball with the Rock Springs Sparklers.

In 1935, Kundla entered the University of Minnesota and joined the freshmen basketball team as a walk-on. A year later he was one of coach Dave MacMillan's starting forwards. MacMillan had played for the Original Celtics and was a tough taskmaster. He utilized a fast break, offensive plays, and man-to-man defense. In the 1936-37 the Gophers tied the University of Illinois for the Big Ten title. By the time Kundla graduated he had made the all-conference team (1938), was the team captain (1939), and led the Gophers in scoring for three consecutive years. After the 1938-39 season Kundla played for the Galloping Gophers and received $25 a game as the Gophers barnstormed throughout the state against the Harlem Globetrotters.

John Kundla

Between 1939 and 1942 Kundla taught physical education at Ascension Elementary School and coached the school's basketball team to three Catholic elementary league championships. He also assisted Dave MacMillan at the University of Minnesota for fifty dollars a month. The men's club at Ascension also sponsored an AAU basketball team which competed in the National AAU Basketball

Tournament in Denver in 1940 and 1941. (Incidentally, 1940 was Jim Pollard's first year at the tournament.) In 1942 Kundla entered the Navy, which took him to the war in the Pacific. After developing a bad case of ulcers, Kundla returned to Minneapolis and resumed his coaching career. He divided his time between DeLaSalle High School, which he led to the state championship in 1944, and assisting MacMillan at the University of Minnesota. In the fall of 1946, Kundla became the head coach at St. Thomas College in St. Paul. He was only 31 years old when Sid Hartman talked him into coaching the Lakers a year later. Little did he know that he was to embark on a journey that would take him to the Hall of Fame.

When Jim and Arilee Pollard moved to Minneapolis, they rented a home with the Napolitanos, Durkees, and John Rocker. During the season, according to Bill Durkee, "we had a game every second or third day and practice if there was no game. It really got to be kind of boring with the severe winter keeping us from doing anything outside." When some friends asked Durkee to go ice fishing, he declined and later admitted that at the time he "couldn't imagine a worse activity." The Californians had to adjust not only to the uncertainties of professional basketball, but also to the harsh Minnesota winters.

The starters for the Lakers' opening game of the 1947-48 season on November 1st were Don Carlson, Don Smith, Bill Durkee, Jim Pollard and Bob Gerber, who had played with the Toledo Jeeps. They won their opener and two of next three. Then they got lucky. On November 13, the Professional Basketball League of America (PBLA) folded. The league was the rather zany idea of Maurice White, owner of the American Gear Company. His Chicago American Gears had competed in the NBL since the 1944-45 season. In March of

"MR. POLLARD, MEET MR. MIKAN"

"The Californians" making a new home in Minneapolis. Paul Napolitano, Arilee Pollard, Nancy Napolitano, Jim Pollard, Mary and Bill Durkee, November 1947.

1946, White had signed George Mikan, DePaul's great All-American center, to a five year contract worth $60,000. In the 1946-47, Mikan led the Gears to an NBL title. Carried away with the Gears success (and also a little greedy) White decided that he could better capitalize on Mikan's fame by pulling the Gears out of the NBL and organizing a new sixteen-team league. The theory was that the Gears, because of Mikan, would draw huge crowds wherever they played and White would rake in the money. His theory was flawed and the league collapsed in a matter of weeks. The Gears tried to get back into the NBL but their application was rejected. The Lakers were particularly vigorous in rejecting the Chicagoan's request because Minneapolis had the first pick in the dispersal draft by virtue of the Detroit Gems last place finish. The Lakers selected Mikan and signed him for $12,500. As a free agent, Mikan could have sold his services to any team in the NBL or BAA. In retrospect, it seems odd that Mikan did not drive a harder bargain. The ease with which this transaction was completed probably reflected the low stature of professional basketball and the absence of agents at that time.

Mikan was born on June 18, 1924, in Joliet, Illinois, to Joseph and Minne Mikan, first-generation Americans who traced their roots to Croatia. George had two brothers, Joe and Ed, and the latter would follow George into the professional basketball arena.

The Mikans, who owned a tavern/restaurant in a poorer part of Joliet, were a closely knit family. As a boy sports and the Catholic church were major influences on Mikan. One of Mikan's most memorable boyhood moments was meeting Babe Ruth at Comiskey Park, an honor won as a result of claiming the Will County marbles championship.

As a freshman at Joliet High School, George failed to make the team because his coach didn't think he could play with glasses. George then went off to Quigley Prep Seminary in Chicago, a school for Catholic boys intent on becoming priests. Although the round trip to Quigley was about 100 miles, Mikan still found time between classes and homework to play basketball in leagues sponsored by the Catholic Youth Organization. In his fourth year in high school, George, now 6'8", played against St. Leo High School, and DePaul University's athletic director, Paul Mattei, offered him a scholarship. In the fall of 1941 George played freshman ball at DePaul. The following year, Ray Meyer, who had starred at Notre Dame, became DePaul's coach. Together Mikan and Meyer would transform DePaul basketball and enjoy careers that would enshrine them in the Basketball Hall of Fame.

In Mikan's first varsity year, 1942-43, DePaul's Blue Demons advanced to the semifinals of the NCAA tournament where they lost to Georgetown 53-49. In 1944 the

Blue Demons lost to St. John's in the finals of the National Invitational Tournament (NIT) at Madison Square Garden.

At that time the NIT was considered the equal of the NCAA as a collegiate tournament. The tournament was the brainchild of Edward "Ned" Irish who was the basketball director and eventually vice-president of Madison Square Garden. Irish brought basketball doubleheaders to the Garden in the 1934-35 season. Their popularity led to the NIT in 1938, one year before the first NCAA tournament. College basketball teams often chose between the tournaments or played in both. In 1945 the Blue Demons elected to return to the NIT and they thumped Bowling Green, 71-54, to win the championship game. In 1945-46 DePaul finished with a 19-5 record but inexplicably was not invited to either the NCAA or the NIT. Mikan finished his DePaul career as a three-time All-American and was named college player of the year twice.

But Mikan was not the only addition to the Lakers roster in the fall of 1947. The dissolution of the Professional Basketball League of America also brought Jack Dwan to the team. A graduate of Chicago's Loyola University, Dwan had started the year with St. Paul in the PBLA. He would quickly secure one of the Lakers' starting guard positions. The Lakers also picked up Herm Schaefer who had distinguished himself on Indiana's 1940 NCAA championship team, with the Great Lakes Naval Training Station during the war, and later with the Fort Wayne Zollner Pistons. Schaefer also earned a starting position, directing the team on the floor from the guard position. Finally, the Lakers added Johnny Jorgenson, who had played at DePaul with Mikan.

To accommodate these additions to the roster, the Laker's were forced to cut Bob Gerber, Bill Durkee, John Rocker, Warren Ajax, and Ken Excel. Almost sixty years later, Kundla recalled that releasing players was the toughest part of his job.

But the pain he felt about giving five players the pink slip may have been assuaged somewhat by the anticipation of having George Mikan, the best center in the country, in the lineup along with Jim Pollard, one of the nation's premier forwards.

For Pollard, the arrival of Mikan posed an interesting dilemma. Up to this point in his career, Pollard had always been the focal point of his team's offense. He had controlled the tempo of the game. At the same time, he had earned a reputation at every level of play for being unselfish. Mikan's presence could limit his creativity, because the offense was going to revolve around the 6'10" center.

All the evidence suggests that the effort to blend the talents of the two stars got off to a rocky start. In 1947, the three second lane was only six feet wide, so Mikan wanted to set up low where he could utilize his hook shot. The problem was that Pollard liked to drive to the basket and now Mikan and his defender clogged up that route, leaving Pollard no room to capitalize on his athleticism. With Mikan in the line-up, the Lakers lost four of its first five games.

Kundla solved the problem, in part, by designing a pick-and-roll play that allowed for some creativity on the part of both players. Mikan also had to make an adjustment. According to Bill Carlson, who wrote for the *Minneapolis Star* at the time, Herm Schaefer took Mikan aside and said, "Look, George, this is the greatest thing that ever happened to you. This Jim Pollard is a great basketball player. He can do anything with that ball, including pass it to you. But you've got to pass it to him, too." Schaefer reminded Mikan, "No matter how big a man you were with the Gears, you can't win these games by yourself."

By the start of the new year, Pollard and Mikan had worked out their differences on the court. Joe Hendrickson of the *Minneapolis Tribune*, wrote: "It must be stated emphatically that Pollard and Mikan are performing brilliantly." Hendrickson thought "Pollard has made a big adjustment in his thinking since turning professional, and while scoring less points than he gained in the first month of the campaign, he had increased his contributions to the Laker cause two-fold." Hendrickson observed that on defense Pollard had an "exceptional ability" to anticipate an opponent's moves, combined with the natural quickness to react in time. As a result, he reported, "Pollard intercepts and bats down enemy shots and passes with regularity." Hendrickson noted that on the other end of the court Pollard frequently passed to teammates who were in better scoring position, "actually sacrificing his own opportunities for points to make a basket more sure no matter who shoots it." Hendrickson concluded, "Pollard is definitely a team man in the present Laker play." All of which is in perfect accord with what we know of how Pollard approached the game of basketball even in his early years on the playgrounds of Oakland.

The style and grace of Pollard's play also captured the attention of other sportswriters. On December 17, after leading the Lakers to a victory over the Toledo Jeeps, Bill Carlson wrote, "That flower of California cagedom, whose blossoms had been wilted by a wretched cold, has begun to bloom. Today it appeared that Jim Pollard was back in the form that made Minneapolis basketball fans probe Webster for new superlatives when they first saw him." On January 18, when the Lakers edged the Rochester Royals on the New Yorker's home court 75-73, George Beahon of the Rochester's *Democrat-Chronicle* wrote, "Besides Mikan, the customers last night saw the fabulous Jim Pollard play his own ball game." Pollard's "spectacular floor play and first half scoring spurt earned him the continual plaudits of the fans."

When the Lakers and Royals met for the third time the venue was the Chicago Stadium. The Lakers prevailed again, with Mikan tallying 23 and Pollard 17. George Beahon thought that Pollard was the star of the game as he "controlled the boards in the second half as though he owned them and drew raves from the crowd because of the manner in which he scored his 17 markers." With Mikan's power and Pollard's athleticism, the Lakers possessed a formidable tandem.

While the Lakers were piling up wins, the Laker organization was thinking about how it could become more profitable. In March, Bill Carlson reported that the Lakers had sold out in 21 of 26 road games, but were averaging only 4,451 fans a game at home, and quite a few of those were guests of the team. As early as January of 1948, the Lakers were exploring the possibility of jumping to the Basketball Association of America. Max Winter believed that Laker fans were not terribly excited by games against Oshkosh, Sheboygan, and Anderson, Indiana. Although a rivalry had developed with the Rochester Royals, Joe Hendrickson thought that even here league rules and scheduling undercut the Lakers' efforts to turn a profitable. They received $500 a game for expenses from the Royals, while paying $750 a game to Rochester; they made three trips to Rochester, though the Royals only made one trip to Minneapolis for two games. Winter was also annoyed when the league allowed Indianapolis to sell Arnie Risen, its center, to Rochester. He argued that the sale upset the league's competitive balance, though he was also well aware that it strengthened a major rival.

Diversions

There were several oddities in the 1947-1948 season as professional basketball worked through its growing pains. One was Pollard's appearance with the College All-Stars against the Indianapolis Kautskys that year. It had been almost six years since he had played for Stanford, and he already had seven professional games under his belt. Nonetheless, he led all players with 19 points as the All-Stars topped the Kautskys 68-62. After the game Dutch Lonborg, coach of the All-Stars, commented, "In the eight years I have been coaching the All-Stars, I have never seen a better player."

Another odd event took place on February 19, 1948, when the Lakers traveled to Chicago Stadium to play the Harlem Globetrotters in a game that has mushroomed in significance with the passage of time. The matchup's origins are a bit murky. According to Ben Green, author of the definitive history of the Globetrotters, the game was scheduled as a result of an item in a column written by Arch Ward, the influential sports editor of the *Chicago Tribune*. With an eye for promoting a game, Ward wrote that the Harlem Globetrotters were the best basketball team in the United States. According to Green, Max Winter, the general manager of the Lakers, disagreed and challenged the Globetrotters to a game.

John Christgau, who has written a book on the game, offers a slightly different version of the story. According to him, more than one writer had dubbed the Globetrotters as the greatest five, and Abe Saperstein, the team's owner-coach, often boasted that the Globetrotters could beat *anybody*. Winter and Saperstein were friends and they both saw the possibilities of a big gate if Winter challenged the Globetrotters to a game.

Known for their ball-handling skills and gags on the court, the Globetrotters were the preeminent barnstorming team of the 1940s. By 1950 they had assembled what was arguably their most talented team. Although a few black players were playing in the professional leagues at the time, until the 1950s Abe Saperstein had the opportunity to sign many of the best African American players in the United States.

One of his most talented players was Marques Haynes. A graduate of Langston University in Oklahoma, Haynes played his first game for the Globetrotters in 1947. For kids growing up at this time, no matter their color, there were two ball-handlers who stood out above everybody—Haynes and Bob Cousy, both of whom were later enshrined in the Hall of Fame. At center, the Globetrotters had Reece "Goose" Tatum, "the clown prince of basketball." At six foot three, Tatum was small for a center, but his long arms and leaping ability compensated for his relative lack of size at that position. Tatum first played for Saperstein in 1941 but lost three years to the service between 1943 and 1945. By 1948 he had no peer as a showman on the court. Ermer Robinson, one of the starting forwards, had developed a sweet one-handed shot as a kid growing up in San Diego. He had starred on the San Diego High School team, and in 1944, following a stint in the service, he helped the Ft. Warren, Wyoming, Broncos to a fourth-place finish in the National AAU Basketball Tournament in Denver. One writer described Robinson as "decidedly a wizard on a basketball floor." Two years later he joined the Globetrotters.

Babe Pressley, the fourth starter, had played for the Globetrotters since 1939. Considered the team's best defensive player, Pressley was given the assignment of guarding Pollard during the game with the Lakers. The fifth starter was Wilbert King, a little guard from Detroit.

The dust jacket copy of John Christgau's *Tricksters in the Madhouse* refers to the Laker-Globetrotters contest as "a game that would encapsulate the growing racial tensions of the era, particularly the struggle of black Americans to gain legitimacy in the segregated world of sports." The claim is made that this "crucial game represented an important step toward equality."

Was the game really that significant? Without a doubt the seeds of the modern civil rights movement were being sown in the 1940s. In 1948, President Harry Truman campaigned in Harlem and the Democratic Party adopted a strong civil rights package at its convention. In 1947, when Jackie Robinson broke the "color line" in major league baseball for the first time, he was in the media's spotlight. Many fans were enthusiastic, and the *Sporting News* gave him its first Rookie of the Year award that year, but Robinson was also the victim of beanball pitches and off-the-field death threats.

The integration of professional basketball took place with far less drama. This was, in part, because it had not yet established itself as an important feature of the American sporting landscape. Nor did the transition have quite so clear-cut a "before" and "after" as Robinson's appearance gave to major league baseball. In 1942-43, a number of Globetrotters worked for the Studebaker Aircraft plant in Chicago and during that time they played on an integrated team. In 1946-47, four African-Americans played in the National Basketball League. One was Dolly King who played for the Rochester Royals. Over the years the Globetrotters played hundreds of white teams, including an annual series with the College

All-Stars. Between 1939 and 1944, the Globetrotters entered the World Professional Basketball Tournament sponsored by the Chicago *Herald-American* and played at the Chicago Stadium. The New York Rens and the Washington Bears were other African-American teams that played in the tournament. In 1948-49, the Dayton Rens played in the National Basketball League.

When the Globetrotters and Lakers met, the Minneapolis team was in its first year and had not yet established itself as the dominant professional team, and there is little evidence to suggest that the game played a pivotal role in the struggle for racial equality. The presence of George Mikan would make any athletic event in Chicago a major attraction, and Winter and Saperstein were anticipating a big payday. Pollard himself later remarked that the game was "for the owners, not the players. I didn't take it seriously…it was a pain in the neck." Another Laker told John Christgau that the players did not "get a cup of coffee" for playing the game. In short, for the Lakers, it was just another game in an already busy schedule. They did not see themselves as representing the white race in some sort of racial drama.

In retrospect, there is something refreshing about the approach of the Laker-Globetrotter players to the game. They knew the score. The game was about business. Winter and Saperstein expected to make some money. The players were under contract to perform as they were told.

Though the encounter perhaps lacks the social significance that has been attributed to it, as an athletic contest it was a resounding success. To the promoters' delight, 17,823 spectators filled the Chicago Stadium to see the two outstanding teams do battle, and few went away disappointed. The Lakers took a 32-23 halftime lead, but the Globetrotters quickly closed the gap in the second half, collapsing on Mikan and hammering him repeatedly on defense. With the game tied at 49, Ermer Robinson hit a long one-hander at the buzzer and the jubilant Globetrotters walked off the stadium floor with a hard-fought victory. In the African American community on Chicago's South Side, black Chicagoans reportedly celebrated into the early hours. Mikan led all scorers with 24 and Pollard followed with 18.

The Lakers and Globetrotters would play six more times between 1949 and 1952 with the Lakers winning five of the games. The two teams did not play again until 1958 when the Lakers added a final victory to their column. The Lakers' continued domination reflected additions to its roster that strengthened the team, while as the integration of professional basketball continued, the Globetrotters found it more difficult to attract the best African American players.

Perhaps the oddest part of the Lakers 1947-48 season came during the playoffs. The Lakers had run away with the Western Division of the NBL with a 43-17 record. Mikan, with a 21.3 average, and Pollard, with 12.8 average, were the only Lakers in double figures for the season. The Lakers breezed by Oshkosh and Tri-Cities in the playoffs, which set up a championship series with their old nemesis the Rochester Royals, who had followed a similar path to the finals in the Eastern Division. But before the two teams met, the Lakers took yet another detour to play in the World Professional Tournament sponsored by the *Chicago Herald American*.

In 1948 this tournament was in the tenth (and last) year of its history. It had always included several NBL teams and at least one of the black traveling teams—often the Harlem Globetrotters or the New York Rens. As usual, the Lakers were merely looking for another payday. After stomping Wilkes-Barre 98-48, they squeezed by the Anderson Duffey Packers 59-56. In the championship game the Lakers faced the New York Rens, who were playing in their tenth consecutive tournament.

During the 1930s the Rens had been the best known of the black barnstorming teams. Organized in 1923 by Robert J. Douglas, a black New Yorker, the Rens played their first game on the ballroom floor of the Renaissance Casino in Harlem. The team originally called itself the Renaissance Big Five. Its 1948 roster included Nat "Sweetwater" Clifton, Roscoe "Duke" Cumberland, William "Pop" Gates and George Crowe—an impressive line-up. On Sunday night April 10, before 17,000 the Lakers squeaked by the Rens 75-71. Mikan poured in 40 points and Pollard followed with 14. Both men earned all-tournament first team honors and Mikan was voted the tournament's MVP.

Champions

Two nights later the Lakers finally met the Rochester Royals in the first game of the best three of five series for the NBL championship. The Royals had entered the NBL in 1945 when Lester "Les" Harrison and his brother, Jack, bought a NBL franchise. Born in Rochester in 1904, Harrison played basketball for that city's East High School. One of his fondest memories was scoring 16 points as a 5'11" center for East in a 20-16 victory over West High School for the city championship.

Even in high school, Harrison had decided that "basketball was going to be my business," and after high school, though he took over the management of his father's fruit and vegetable business, basketball remained his passion. During his free time Harrison began to organize, coach, and play on semipro teams in the Rochester area. In 1940, Harrison's Rochester Seagrams were good enough to be invited to the World Basketball

Tournament. Without his energy and promotional skills, professional basketball might never have come to Rochester.

As a coach, Harrison was not a technician in the modern sense of that term. Bill Calhoun, who was a rookie with the Royals in 1947-48, could not recall Harrison offering any instruction whatsoever. He relied on his players to make suggestions regarding tactics and strategy, though he took it upon himself to make player substitutions and he freely exercised his right to argue with officials.

A number of the Royals were from New York City and they worked up a motion offense that emphasized moving without the ball. Though Harrison was not a technician, the team appreciated his energy, and several who played for him later recalled that Harrison "genuinely loved his players." When Harrison approached his 93rd birthday, Calhoun received a call from him just to ask how he was doing. Harrison was a life-long bachelor, and it's likely that he considered the team his "family."

Harrison's most experienced player was Al Cervi, a hard-driving guard who earned the nickname "Digger" for his tenacious defensive play. Cervi had been an all-sports star at East High School in Buffalo, New York. After graduating in 1936, Cervi chose to work and play semipro basketball rather than attend college. He hooked up with Les Harrison in 1937 when the latter was managing and coaching a Rochester team sponsored by Eber Brothers, a liquor distributor. Except for 1942-45, when the Air Force transferred him from Niagara Falls to Foster Field, Texas, Cervi was a fixture in Rochester basketball. At 5'11" and 195 lbs, he was extremely strong. He liked to take his defender into the pivot drive and pick up a foul and the three-point play. Bill Calhoun remembered that he usually came through in the clutch. When the game was close Calhoun's first thought was to get the ball to Cervi.

The Cervi-Harrison connection ended in a contract dispute following the 1947-48 season. Cervi moved on to Syracuse, where he was successful both as a player and coach until he retired from the sport in 1955.

One of the most polished of the Royals was Bobby Davies. A native of Harrisburg, Pennsylvania, Davis blossomed at Seton Hall where he played for John "Honey" Russell. Davies was later credited with being one of the first players to dribble behind his back. At 6'2", he had a complete game and loved the fast break. As a college player Davies so impressed Clair Bee that the Long Island coach used him as a model for his Chip Hilton series. With his long blonde hair, he was the picture of the All-American boy.

Jim scores against Bob Wanzer of the Rochester Royals.

After graduating in 1942, Davies enlisted in the Navy and made the All-Service team with Great Lakes Naval Station in 1943. After serving for two years as an officer on an anti-submarine chaser, Les Harrison signed Davies to a contract, and the "Harrisburg Houdini" soon became one of his favorite players. Harrison recalled, "I paid him a $1000 a month. I gave him a bonus the following year and I signed him up for four years on a hand shake." Davies controlled the tempo of the game for the Royals and was a perennial all-star. He was elected to the Basketball Hall of Fame in 1969.

Between 1945 and 1947, Davies coached Seton Hall's baseball and basketball teams while commuting from

Rochester. One of his players was Bobby Wanzer, a future Hall of Famer. A clever guard and an outstanding shooter from both the field and foul line, Wanzer was a product of New York City basketball. He grew up in East Harlem and led Benjamin Franklin High School to city championships in 1940 and 1941. During World War II Wanzer served in the Marines, returning to Seton Hall for the 1946-1947 season. Harrison drafted Wanzer in 1947 and the scrappy guard would play ten years for him, earning all-NBA honors three times. Wanzer had a variety of shots, seldom made mistakes with the ball, and was good defensively.

Rounding out Harrison's stable of guards was William "Red" Holzman. Best known as the coach of the New York Knicks from 1967 through 1977, Holzman grew up in Brooklyn. In 1942 and 1943, Holzman played for Nat Holman at CCNY. After two years in the Navy, he signed with the Royals in 1945, where he earned a reputation as a tenacious defender and made the NBL All-Star team three times. In 1986 Holzman entered the Hall of Fame as a coach.

In mid-season the Royals, who needed a big man to counter Mikan, purchased 6'9" Arnie Risen. A native of Williamstown, Kentucky, Risen had played college ball for Harold Olsen at Ohio State in 1944 and 1945, when the Buckeye teams made it to the semifinals of the NCAA tournament two years running. In the latter year he scored 26 in a semifinal loss to New York University. Risen left Ohio State during the 1945-46 season and signed a professional contract with the Indianapolis Kautskys. He had a beautiful hook shot with either hand and ran the court well at 6' 9".

At Indianapolis Risen really learned how to play basketball. His first coach there was Nat Hickey, whose pro basketball resume reached back into the mid-1920s. Hickey drilled Risen on a player's responsibility to screen out the man he was guarding on an offensive shot and expounded on what a player was supposed to do when he didn't have the basketball. When the Kautskys were on the road, Risen and Hickey roomed together, and Risen later recalled that Hickey talked incessantly about basketball. (Risen would join Bobby Davies and Wanzer in the Basketball Hall of Fame in 1998.)

Against Mikan, Risen's only disadvantage was that he weighed 210 pounds, about 50 pounds less than the Laker star. But unfortunately for Risen and the Royals, in a semifinal game against the Anderson Packers, Howie Schultz, the Packers' center, accidentally clipped Risen with an elbow and broke the big center's jaw in two places. He never appeared in the final series.

Jim takes a shot above the outstretched hand of Arnie Risen

With Risen out, the Royals had to rely on George Ratkovicz and Arnie Johnson to contain Mikan. Like Cervi, Ratkovicz had not attended college. His professional career began with the Chicago Bruins in 1940 and included a stop with the Chicago Gears and Tri-Cities. At 6' 6" and 220 pounds, the bulky Ratkovicz still gave away size and strength to Mikan. Arnie Johnson was a native of Gonvick, Minnesota, who played had his college ball at Bemidji State. At six feet and five inches, Johnson weighed 240 pounds and was reputed to be incredibly strong. He played tough defense and set excellent screens for Rochester's guards with his wide body. The Royals also hoped to get some scoring from Andy Duncan, a 6' 6" forward who weighed 195 pounds. Duncan had played his college ball at William and Mary and the University of Kentucky, and also had AAU experience.

The finals opened at the Minneapolis Armory rather than the Minneapolis Auditorium, the Lakers home court, because the circus happened to be in town. The players didn't like the Armory floor, which was made of tightly jetted wood blocks over a marble base, and had little or no "spring."

With Risen already on the sidelines due to injury, the Royals chances suffered a second blow when they learned that an injury to Cervi would also keep him out of the game. The Lakers took the first game 80-72 before a standing room only crowd of 8,143, the largest ever to see a game at the Armory. The crowd impressed columnist Charles Johnson who wrote: "The turnout for the Lakers and Rochester Tuesday night settled the future of basketball in this city. It's here to stay. In fact it probably will develop into the most popular winter sport we have in Minneapolis in years to come." The next night five Lakers hit for double figures and the Lakers dominated the Royals 82-67.

At that point the series shifted to Rochester and the Royals won game three rather easily, 74-60, with a standout performance by Bill Calhoun, a 19-year-old rookie who had played the previous season with Pollard on the Oakland Bittners. Calhoun, who had spent most of his time on the bench during the season, not only scored 13 but held Pollard to three.

There was a touch of irony in Calhoun's success against Pollard. The young Royal had graduated from San Francisco's Lowell High School where he played for the legendary Benny Neff. Seven years younger than Pollard, Calhoun recalled that Jim was "the player we all emulated in the schoolyard."

When Calhoun skipped college to play for the Bittners, Jim's friendliness made the transition easy. In the 1947 National AAU tournament, Calhoun made the AAU All-America team. "When I ran onto the court to receive my plaque," he wrote, "I remember seeing that he was almost as happy as I was." Les Harrison saw the 1947 tournament and signed Calhoun to a contract.

In the fourth game of the series, however, Calhoun lost his battle with Pollard, who scored 19 to add to Mikan's 27 as the Lakers took the series three games to one.

After the game Bob Davies, analysing the Laker team, attributed 60 percent of the Lakers' strength to Mikan. Without Mikan, Davies added, "50 percent of the club would be Jim Pollard." But Mikan clogged up the area around the basket, limiting Pollard's ability to drive to the basket. Jim Peterson, writing for the *Minnesota Sunday Tribune*, noted: "In the last half, it was Pollard all over the floor, sailing up near the rim of the basket time after time for rebounds and for tip-ins." Kundla thought the Lakers had played "our greatest game" of the season. Rochester offered no excuses, but clearly an interesting rivalry had been born. The nine Lakers who had competed split up a pool of money totaling $9,308.86 for the entire playoffs.

Pollard finished sixth in the NBL in scoring that year with a 12.9 average per game. Marko Todorovich of Sheboygan nosed him out for rookie-of-year honors, 22 votes to 20. They both made the all NBL's first team along with Mikan, "Red" Holzman, and Al Cervi. After the season Pollard was asked how he felt about playing with Mikan. One of the advantages, he said, was that he played "with less pressure than I ever had."

During the off-season Maurice Podoloff, in his untiring efforts to end the bidding war for players that plagued the rival leagues, lured three NBL teams into the BAA. Fort Wayne and Indianapolis were the first to jump. This initial success gave Podoloff a little momentum and sent a message to the NBL, warning it that its days were numbered. But the real prize, in Podoloff's estimation, was the Lakers, because with Mikan on the floor they were always a big draw. Since the home team kept all the gate receipts, every Laker visit would be a good payday. The Laker's owner, Ben Berger, was eager for his team to play in bigger cities, and he had little difficulty deciding to make the switch. Once the Lakers jumped, Les and Jack Harrison insisted that the Rochester Royals also be included in the new set-up.

The addition of the Lakers and Royals gave the BAA a significant talent infusion, though oddly enough, both teams were placed in the Western Division. Each division now had six teams, and all the teams were scheduled to play a sixty game schedule.

In 1948 the Lakers added Arnie Ferrin from Utah and Don Forman from New York University. Ferrin's roots ran deep into Utah's history, his great-grandfather having arrived with Brigham Young when the Mormons settled the territory in 1847. Several generations later, Arnie Ferrin, at 6'4" and 165 pounds, walked-on at the University of Utah in the fall of 1943. The armed services had drained Vadal Peterson's Utes of upperclassmen and the veteran coach played the season with five freshmen and a sophomore. After losing in the first round of the 1944 NIT to Kentucky, Utah was about to return to Salt Lake City when it learned that Arkansas could not accept its bid to the NCAA tournament because several players had been injured in an automobile accident. Utah was offered the slot and headed to Kansas City, where it defeated

Jim and Arnie Ferrin enjoy a friendly game of pool.

Missouri and Iowa State in the tournament's opening rounds. At that point the Utes headed back to Madison Square Garden to play Dartmouth for the NCAA Championship. Ferrin poured in 22 points as Utah squeaked by Dartmouth 42-40 in overtime. Ferrin was the first freshman named MVP of the tournament, a distinction he held until 1986 when Pervis Ellison led Louisville to an NCAA title.

During the war, the NCAA and NIT champions played each other at Madison Square Garden to raise money for the Red Cross, and Utah ended its remarkable season a few days later by defeating St. John's University 43-36.

After two years in the service Ferrin resumed his career in 1946-47. In his first year back he teamed up with Vern Gardner to lead Utah over Kentucky, 49-45, to win the NIT tournament. After the 1947-48 season the Lakers made the four-time All-American their first round draft choice. An NBL team offered Ferrin more money, but the chance to play with a champion was too much to resist. After playing several months with the Lakers, Ferrin thought: "This is the closest thing to a college team that I've ever seen.... There are no jealousies on our squad because Mikan and Pollard make the largest salaries and score the most points."

The Laker's second roster addition, Don Forman, was born in the Brownsville section of Brooklyn on January 17, 1926. His mother died when he was in junior high school and he and his father, Mike, lived with his aunt and her husband during his teenage years. In the fall of 1941, Forman entered Boys High School in the middle of Brooklyn's Bedford – Stuyvesant neighborhood. Boys High was an open enrollment school which at one time had a reputation for academic excellence. Boys from all over the city commuted to Bed-Sty for an education. By 1941 Boys High was almost fifty percent black and the neighborhood was becoming less inviting.

The educational history of Boys High mattered little to Forman. By his own admission he was not a good student, but he had a passion for basketball. Mickey Fisher was the coach at Boys High and well on his way to becoming a legend in New York City high school basketball circles. Although Fisher spent the war years in the armed services, this did not slow down Forman. In his senior year, he earned a spot on the All-City first team, scored 49 points in one game, and was the city's high scorer. Despite these honors, Forman had no scholarship offers. At 5'10" and 150 pounds, college coaches probably looked at him as just another good "little man."

Forman found his way to New York University in the strangest way. His best high school friend and teammate was Burton "Buddy" Monasch. If Forman was an indifferent student, Monasch was something of a genius. Monasch suggested that they enroll at New York University. The NYU gym and athletic facilities were uptown around 181st street, and Monasch and Forman went up to the athletic facilities one day in the spring of 1944 to look for Howard Cann, the NYU's basketball coach. They found him watching a baseball game. Monasch said, according to Forman, "I am Buddy Monasch and this is Don Forman. We would like to play basketball at NYU." Cann proceeded to take them into his office and called the downtown campus to arrange for their registration. Forman's scholarship covered his tuition and he lived at home for his four years at NYU.

NYU had outstanding teams during Forman's four years with the Violets. In his freshman year, Forman started on a team with Sid Tanenbaum and Dolph Schayes that lost in the NCAA finals Oklahoma A & M. In his senior year NYU lost in the finals of the National Invitational Tournament to Ed Macauley's St. Louis Billikens.

Forman's assessment of the Lakers matched that of Arnie Ferrin's. The team was closely knit. Pollard and Mikan "set themselves above everybody else. They were there to win." He marveled at how Pollard controlled the boards. Mikan was "bigger than life." After playing New York basketball, Forman remembered that he had to adjust to an offense with set plays for Mikan and Pollard. He liked John Kundla, whom he described as "a mild-mannered gentleman."

As the 1948-49 season entered March, the Lakers were locked in a tough Western Division race with the Rochester Royals and Chicago Stags. Before the season ended, the Lakers sandwiched in two games with the Harlem Globetrotters. On the last day of February, the Lakers, without an injured Pollard and Carlson, lost to the Globetrotters for the second time, 49-45, before 20,046 at the Chicago Stadium. Two weeks later the Lakers drubbed the Globetrotters 68-53, as a record 10,122 jammed into the Minneapolis Auditorium. Mikan poured in 32 and Pollard had seven assists and nine points. Two weeks earlier, Marques Haynes had put on a dribbling show after the Globetrotters had built up a comfortable lead. Don Forman reciprocated for the Lakers that night, offering

The Lakers arrive in Chicago for the playoffs. Top: Don Forman, Herm Schaefer, Swede Carlson (hat), Jack Dwan, Arnie Ferrin, Whitey Kahan, Bud Grant. Standing: John Kundla, George Mikan, Tony Jaros, flight attendant, Jim Pollard, ballboy, Earl Gardiner, Johnny Jorgensen.

a dribbling demonstration which, according to one writer, "rivaled the show Marques Haynes put on in Chicago."

Fifty-seven years later, Forman still had a vivid memory of the evening. He said that he had never had done such a thing before, and was not trying to show off. But when the Trotter players started chasing him, he spontaneously kept the ball. Forman also downplayed the significance of the race factor in those games against the Trotters, pointing out that he had often played with and against black players in Brooklyn.

Although the Lakers posted an impressive 44-16 record that year, it was not good enough to clinch the division title. The Royals finished one game ahead of them. In the first round of the playoffs, the Lakers met the Chicago Stags, led by high-scoring Max Zaslofsky and two of the University of Illinois' celebrated whiz kids, Andy Phillip and Gene Vance. Although the playoffs opened at home, the Lakers, according to Glen Gaff of the *Minneapolis Morning Tribune*, looked "jittery," and they trailed at the half by two. Pollard's play," Gaff added, "was about the only bright sport of the entire first half." The Lakers eventually won 84-77, and they finished off Chicago the following night with a resounding 101-85 victory.

The victory meant that Minneapolis would tangle with Rochester in the Western Division finals. Since the Royals had won the Western Division, the first game was played in Rochester's Edgerton Park Arena, which only seated 4200. The Lakers blew a seventeen-point lead during the second half but Tony Jaros hit a clutch basket with eighteen seconds left to tie the game. An Arnie Ferrin free throw at the six-second mark gave the Lakers a slim 80-79 victory.

A few days later in Minneapolis the Lakers cinched the series 67-55, in a defensive battle in which they kept the Royals from scoring a field goal in the fourth quarter. Mikan was high man with 31 points.

In the BAA finals, the Lakers met the Washington Capitols, who were coached at that time by the formidable Arnold "Red" Auerbach. Auerbach had played high school ball in New York City and his college basketball at George Washington University. After coaching several high school teams, "Red" served in the Navy for three years. While in the Navy, Auerbach coached a basketball team composed of Washington Redskins football players. The Redskins played some of their games in Mike Uline's arena. Uline had been one of the sports businessmen involved in the formation of the BAA in 1946, and Auerbach persuaded Uline to hire him as the Capitols first coach.

The Capitals entered the finals that year without the on-court presence of Bob Feerick, who had been one of their high scorers during the season. Jack Nichols, Horace "Bones" McKinney, Fred Scolari, Sonny Hertzberg, and Kleggie Hermsen were some of the players that Auerbach relied upon to compete with the Lakers.

The Lakers captured the first game of the best-of-seven series, 88-84, with Mikan racking up 42 points; after the game Auerbach predicted glibly: "We'll win the series if we can take that one Wednesday." But the Lakers overpowered the Capitols once again on Wednesday, 76-62, before a record crowd of 10,212 at the Minneapolis Auditorium. The Capitols succeeded in hold down Mikan's rampant scoring, limiting him to 10 points by double- and triple-teaming him, but this inevitably freed up the other Lakers and Pollard, Schaefer, and Carlson all hit for double figures. Glen Gaff reported that "the Caps never had a chance on the backboards. Pollard played them like he owned them."

When the series moved to Washington, the Lakers continued their dominance with a 94-74 victory. Finally, in game four, the Capitals snapped their losing streak with an easy 83-71 victory, Jack Nichols leading the Caps with 27 points. After the game, x-rays disclosed that Mikan had chipped a bone in his right wrist. He continued to lead the Laker scorers the following night while playing with a taped wrist, but the Caps came away with a 74-65 victory.

Finally, in front of a home-town crowd at the St. Paul Auditorium, the Lakers buried the Caps once and for all, 77-56, to win the championship. Mikan poured in 29 points and three other Lakers reached double figures. The Caps were never close. For finishing second in the league, winning the playoffs and the championship the Lakers split $13,000.

Above: Jim and Arilee in their first new home.

Bottom: Tres Ferrin, Jack Pollard, and Larry and Terry Mikan accompany their dads to the First National Bank, October 1949.

Mikan had a monster season in 1948-1949, averaging 28 points per game and 30 per game in the playoffs. Pollard averaged 14.8 per game, and the two were named to the All-BAA first team. Joe Hendrickson felt that Pollard's all-around game had surpassed the previous year," and he noted that when Pollard left the floor near the end of the final game of the BAA championship series, "the applause Jim received was a true expression of the customer's appreciation of the skill he showed them during the season."

After the season, Jim and Arilee decided to make Minneapolis their year-around home. Their first child, Jack, had been born the previous May, and the family would grow to four when Jeanne was born in August of 1950. Meanwhile, Jim enrolled at the University of Minnesota where he eventually finished his college degree.

Looking back on that era, Jim later expressed the view that "in the professional game the job of being able to get along is harder than in college." He had become convinced that "common sense and some individual sacrifice" were crucial to Laker success. The combination produced more victories, which meant, in turn, that the players made more money.

But in the early years of professional basketball, the financial rewards of even an all-star player on a championship team were extremely modest. For example, in the spring of 1949, the BAA sent Pollard a check for $200 for being named to the All-Star team. During the playoffs, the BAA assumed the costs of "the actual train fare, hotel expenses, and the cost of meals for not exceeding 10 players, and a coach per team." The league stated that each player would be allotted a $5.00 per diem for meals and $3.50 a day for a hotel room. In order to make ends meet while raising a family and pursuing a college degree, Jim played semi-professional baseball during the summer with a team in Jordan, Minnesota.

4
The Lakers Tackle the NBA

"Pollard could float through the air like Julius Irving and Michael Jordan."

– Laker teammate Bob Harrison

By the 1949-50 season, the "Jim Pollard" style of play was well established and it caught the eye of teammates, opponents, journalists and fans alike. Dick Cullum, writing for the *Minneapolis Morning Tribune*, wrote: "Players on the visitors' bench just sit there and shake their heads when the Lakers' Jim Pollard turns on the heat." In comparing Jim to athletes in other sports, Cullum thought there were "not many showings of super ability in any field of sport than can approach a Jim Pollard burst." Howie Schultz, who played both with and against Jim, said the same thing differently: "Jim Pollard was the best player in the league, when he wanted to be." Vince Boryla, who guarded Pollard in AAU ball and then as a New York Knick, recalled: "He was hell on wheels."

Jim's teammates and opponents agreed that he was especially tough in Minneapolis. In basketball there is always a home court advantage, but for Jim there was a special incentive—Arilee. She was often called The Voice of the Lakers.

Blessed with a piercing voice and no inhibitions about using it, she was described by Don Forman, for one, as a "screamer." He added, "Jim Pollard was her life."

Cedric Adams, a popular voice on WCCO radio and a columnist for the *Minneapolis Morning Tribune*, once noted that Arilee sat in section five about the ninth row, and "heaven protect the official if he calls a bum decision." One night, when she vociferously questioned one of referee Sid Borgia's calls, he replied "You are in fine voice tonight, Mrs. Pollard." "Sure I can hear her when I'm playing," Jim admitted. "But she doesn't yell at the opposition. She just roots for us and me."

During the years of the Lakers' great success in Minneapolis, writers were fond of exploring the relationship between Pollard and Mikan. While Jim admitted that the two stars had their differences on the court, they never allowed that to affect their relationship off the court. Moreover, Pollard admitted, "I couldn't stand the pressure of being the key man for seventy games in one season. Neither could he." The bottom line was winning. Pollard once remarked, "Playing with Mikan means you're on a winning team. A winner makes more money and enjoys his work more."

In 1949-50, professional basketball experienced another of its many permutations. On August 3, 1949, the competition between the BAA and NBL was resolved when the two leagues merged to form the seventeen-team National Basketball Association (NBA). The NBA was divided into three divisions: Eastern, Central, and Western. All of the NBA Western Division teams were from the NBL except the Indianapolis Olympians. The Indiana team was built around University of Kentucky All-Americans who had won back-to-back NCAA championships in 1948-49. The key players were Alex Groza, Ralph Beard, Cliff Barker, Wallace "Wah Wah" Jones, and Joe Holland. The only NBL team to play outside the Western Division was the Syracuse Nationals, which played in the Eastern Division.

The new league was an awkward mix of large and small cities. At one extreme was Ned Irish, president and director of Madison Square Garden. Irish wanted the NBA to become a big-time draw and had little patience for the smaller franchises. While the other teams recognized that the inclusion of New York City was a key to the NBA's success, they also envied Irish's financial resources and resented his arrogant manner. At the other extreme, both financially and geographically, was the Denver Nuggets. Managed by Hal Davis, the Nuggets had no financial resources to draw on other than gate receipts.

The Lakers had been placed in the NBA's Central Division along with Rochester, Fort Wayne, Chicago and St. Louis. In the fall of 1949, as they prepared to make a run at their third consecutive championship (each in a different league!), the Lakers began to reap the benefits of an unusually productive draft which had brought Vern Mikkelsen, Slater Martin, and Bob Harrison to the roster.

The team's first round draft choice that year was Vern Mikkelsen, a 6' 7", 230 pound forward from Hamline University. Born on October 21, 1928, in the town of Parlier, in California's Central Valley, Vern had moved with his family to Withee, Wisconsin, before his first birthday. Vern's father was a minister in the Danish Lutheran Church and the family moved several more times before settling in Askov, Minnesota, whose population at the time was 350. Vern was "discovered" by a scouting agent from Hamline while at work in a rutabaga field outside town following his senior year at Askov High, and he received a scholarship to play at Hamline for the next four years.

When Mikkelsen arrived on campus in the fall, his first exposure to Piper basketball was Howie Schultz. In 1942, Schultz had led the Pipers to the National Association of Intercollegiate Basketball Championship (NAIB) in Kansas City. Schultz later became one of the few athletes to play both baseball and basketball at the major league level. In the fall of 1945, while Joe Hutton was in Europe giving basketball clinics, Shultz's assignment was to refine Mikkelsen's skills at the center position. They worked well together and would eventually become teammates and life long friends.

Hamline competed in the Minnesota Intercollegiate Athletic Association, but it had a national reputation and also played a big-time schedule outside the conference. In Mikkelsen's four years he would play against schools like Wyoming, DePaul, and Minnesota. The schedule attracted talented players like Schultz, Rollie Seltz, and John Norlander all of whom went on to play professional basketball. The tough schedule paid off in 1949 when Hamline won its second NAIB championship. Following this memorable season, Mikkelsen traveled to New York to play in the East-West College All-Star Game. Against some of the top college talent in the nation Mikkelsen led all scorers with 17 points. He was recruited by Phillips 66, but decided to stay in Minneapolis.

Although an All-American and a first round choice, Mikkelsen's bargaining leverage was limited by the fact that Hamline was not a big-time program. According to Joe Hutton, Jr., when Mikkelsen met with Max Winter to talk contract, he did not have a lawyer. Instead, Mikkelsen's coach, Joe Hutton, and Mikkelsen's father accompanied him. Winter was a tough negotiator. When Mikkelsen and Winter got to the bottom line, Mik turned to his father and said "What do you think, Dad?" His father replied in a way that suggested that Winter had the upper hand. "Well, money isn't everything." With the Lakers Mikkelsen soon won the forward position opposite Pollard. Although not yet called the "power forward," Mikkelsen became the prototype for that position.

Mikkelsen and Pollard soon found they had something in common besides their position. They both liked to sing. They soon got accustomed to singing the national anthem in two-part harmony before games, taking turns with the lead and harmony, and later critiquing one another's performance. During the 1950-51 season they even formed a quartet with Tony Jaros and Kevin O'Shea.

From the University of Texas the Lakers added 5'10" Slater Martin. Born on October 22, 1925, in El Mina, Texas, Martin's parents separated when he was two, and Martin spent his childhood in Houston, Texas, under the eye of his grandmother, Mrs. J. H. Sheppard. When Slater showed an interest in basketball, Mrs. Sheppard asked Slater's uncle to put up a hoop in the backyard along with lights so that he could shoot baskets and work on his game. As a 5 foot 7 inch guard with great quickness, Martin helped Jefferson Davis High School, coached by Roy Needham, win state championships in 1942 and 1943. Later Martin would praise Needham as "one of the best basketball coaches who ever lived. It was unheard of back then to coach fundamentals the way he did."

In the fall of 1943, Martin enrolled at the University of Texas—the only school to offer him a scholarship. When he turned eighteen, rather than waiting to be drafted, Martin enlisted in the Navy. In the fall of 1946, Martin returned to the University of Texas where he played for three years under Jack Gray, an outstanding athlete at Texas and excellent bas-

The first live television show in Minneapolis. Arnie Ferrin, Herb Schaeffer, Joey Hutton, Dugie Martin, Bob Harrison, Ed Beach, Tony Jaros, Jim, Kevin O'Shea and Vern Mikkelsen (Mikan was being interviewed).

ketball coach. Martin was no stranger to success or big games. In 1947, the Longhorns won the Southwest Conference but fell to Oklahoma in the semifinals of the NCAA tournament, 55-54. On that night Martin led all scorers with 18. The following year the Longhorns lost in the semifinals of the NIT to New York University 45-43. In his senior year, Martin scored 49 points against Texas Christian University and finished his career with several Longhorn scoring records.

Phillips Petroleum Company recruited Martin, but when he learned he that he would have to spend every day behind a desk, he decided to sign with the Lakers for $5000. Only later did he read the fine print, which stipulated that $1500 of his salary would come from the playoffs and was not guaranteed. More than a little annoyed with this sleight of hand, in later years Martin would become an annual holdout.

Perhaps the Laker management regretted being so chary

in their dealings with "Dugie" (as he was being called by then) when they found out what an accomplished athlete they had acquired. Martin was quick and he could run all day. When point guard Herm Schaefer suffered an injury in mid-season Martin joined the starting line-up and performed brilliantly in the position, bringing the ball up the court, triggering the offense, and playing tight defensive.

The Lakers found another nugget in the 1949 draft when they plucked Bob Harrison from the University of Michigan. Like Pollard, Kundla, and Martin, Bob Harrison grew up the hard way. He was born on August 12, 1927, in Indianapolis, Indiana. When he was two years old, his father, a full-blooded Winnebago Indian, was killed. Following his father's death, his mother moved to Toledo, Ohio, where Harrison grew up. When Harrison was nine years old, Dorr Wilkinson, the athletic director at a recreational center sponsored by Big Brothers, invited him to jump into a basketball game. He did, scored a couple baskets, and was hooked on the game. In one grade school game Bob scored 139 points which earned him a citation in *Ripley's Believe It Or Not*.

At Woodward High School Harrison was coached by Homer Hanham, who had established himself as one of the best coaches in Ohio. By his junior year, Harrison had become a powerfully built 6' 2", 185-pound forward. Two of his teammates, Johnny Payak and Paul Seymour also went on to play professionally. The latter would become a lifelong friend. In 1944, this trio helped Woodward win the city championship and reach the finals of the state tournament in Columbus, where they lost in overtime to Middletown. In 1945, Woodward was undefeated in the regular season but lost in district play when Seymour was out with the measles. In 1944 and 1945, Harrison earned first team All-City and All-State honors.

In the fall of 1945, Harrison entered the University of Michigan. One of Michigan's attractions was that its Ann Arbor campus was only fifty miles from Toledo, which made it easy for Harrison's mother to attend the games. In Harrison's junior year, the Wolverines (coached by Ozzie Cowles) won the Big Ten title and earned a bid to the NCAA tournament, though they lost in the first round to Holy Cross led by Bob Cousy and George Kaftan. In his senior year, Harrison captained the Wolverines and won first team All Big Ten honors. He played in the East-West College All Star game in Madison Square Garden that year, where two of his teammates were Vern Mikkelson and Slater Martin.

Harrison's rookie contract with the Lakers was for $3,750. Harrison fit in easily and loved playing for the Lakers because the team was closely knit and there were few controversies. He was a special favorite of the Twin Cities' Native American community. During the summers he sponsored and played with an all-Indian softball team. The only racial incident he could remember from those years took place after one of the softball games, when he took the team to a local bar and the owner refused to serve the team, though he said he would serve Harrison. Harrison avoided a confrontation by buying a keg of beer and inviting the team to his home for a post-game party.

Before he left Minneapolis, Harrison played on three of the Laker championship teams. Slater Martin described him as a "big, strong kid—a real good player." Thinking back on the time he spent on the court with Pollard, Harrison remembered his teammate as "the prototype forward as a shooter, rebounder, passer and floor leader." He recalled that Jim "perfected a hook pass into Mikan...that was virtually impossible to defend." When the Lakers were on the fast break, Jim "had a fake pass that invariably made the defensive player leave his

The 1949 Lakers: Coach John Kundla, Herm Schaefer, Jack Dwan, George Mikan, Arnie Ferrin, Jim Pollard

position to follow the pass, leaving Jim open for an uncontested lay-up." Pollard was also adept at starting a fast break off a defensive rebound and hitting a teammate who was streaking up the court unopposed. Pollard was the first player Harrison had seen who could take off at the top of the circle and make a lay-up without traveling. According to Harrison, Pollard "could float through the air like…Julius Irving and Michael Jordan." He was also impressed with Pollard's anticipation and timing on defense. But in Harrison's eyes Pollard was more than simply a graceful athlete. He was also an outstanding teammate. "Jim was instrumental in giving me confidence and helping me to adjust to the professional style of play," he recalled.

One of the more memorable games of the 1949-50 season (or any Laker season), took place on December 14th against the Knicks. The marquee in front of Madison Square Garden read "Mikan vs. Knicks." In the locker room before the game, Mikan, who was extremely near-sighted, failed to observe that his teammates were not getting dressed, and when he put his glasses on he was surprised to see that they were still in street clothes. He asked what was going on, and Slater Martin replied that the marquee out front said it was Mikan v. Knicks. "Go get'em," Martin said. Everybody had a big laugh.

As in the previous two seasons, the Lakers took time out from league play to renew their rivalry with the Harlem Globetrotters, but the Laker lineup had changed considerably since their last match-up. In particular, the presence of Mikkelsen in place of "Swede" Carlson at forward now made it possible for the Lakers to dominate the boards at both ends of the court. The Globetrotters had the same starting lineup—Ermer Robinson, "Goose" Tatum, "Sweatwater" Clifton, Marques Haynes, and "Babe" Pressley—that had given them a 2-1 advantage in the rivals' first three meetings.

Dugie Martin, who was playing in his first game against the Globetrotters, recalled that the game was important to the Lakers. There was pride involved. And on February 21, 1951, before 21,666 fans at the Chicago Stadium, they dominated the Globetrotters 76-60. Mikan, Mikkelsen, and Pollard scored 36, 13, and 12 respectively. A month later in St. Paul, Mikan, Mikkelsen, and Pollard tallied 21, 18, and 16, respectively, in a no less convincing 69-54 win. Marques Haynes with 23 was the top scorer for the Trotters.

The Lakers and Royals ended the 1950 season of league play with identical 51-17 records. A coin flip decided that the game to determine the league champion would be played in Rochester on March 21, the day after the second Globetrotter game. On Rochester's home court the Lakers played well, and with less than a minute left to play and the score tied at 76, they had the ball. Playing for the last shot, the plan was to feed Mikan for a bucket or perhaps a foul in the act of shooting. When the Royals denied the entry pass, Pollard was forced to release the ball to Tony Jaros in the back court who hit a long shot to give the Lakers a big 68-66 victory.

After defeating Rochester, the Lakers beat Chicago, Ft. Wayne, and the Anderson Packers without losing a game to reach the finals against the Syracuse Nationals.

Their owner, Danny Biasone, was, like Ben Berger, an immigrant success story. His family had arrived in America from Italy in 1919, when Biasone was ten years old. As a kid Biasone loved to play golf, football, and baseball. His father, a conductor for the Syracuse Transit Lines, encouraged these pursuits, telling him, "You play sports and you won't end up in jail." Eventually Biasone owned several bowling alleys and a restaurant which enabled him to buy a franchise in the NBL for $6000. He called the team the Nationals because "I had the hope that someday this team would be the national champion."

The Nationals played at the State Fair Coliseum. Their player-coach was the feisty Al Cervi, and their high scorer was Dolph Schayes, a perennial NBA All Star. Schayes had played his college ball at New York University for Howard Cann between 1945 and 1949. At 6'7," Schayes could play outside, utilizing an excellent two-hand set shot, but he could also drive to the basket. Other notable Nats were George Ratkovicz, Johnny Macknowski, Alex Hannum, Paul Seymour, and Bill Gabor. Al Cervi later recalled the season as the most pleasant of his life. Because of Biasone, the Nats traveled first class, stayed at the best hotels and ate good meals.

Syracuse had won the home court advantage by virtue of having posted the best regular season record (51-13). Near the end of the first game, Bud Grant (who would later end a stellar professional sports career as head coach of the

Minnesota Vikings) scored his only basket to tie the score at 66. Syracuse stalled for the last shot, but Al Cervi failed to connect on a driving lay-up, and Pollard directed the outlet pass to Bobby Harrison, who hit a forty-footer just before the final buzzer to give the Lakers the victory. Mikan tallied 37 for a new record on the Syracuse court and Pollard added 14, the only other Laker in double figures.

After the game someone mentioned to the press corps that the smoke in the State Fair Coliseum, where the game had been played, bothered Mikan. The following night the Syracuse crowd came armed with cigars and filled the coliseum with smoke, which perhaps helped the Nationals pulled out a 91-85 win.

Since neither the Minneapolis Auditorium nor Arena were available, the next two games were played at the St. Paul Auditorium. With Mikan, Mikkelsen and Pollard scoring 28, 27, and 13, respectively, the Lakers outscored the Nats 49-38 in the second half to post a 91-77 victory. The reported crowd of 10,288 fans set a new attendance record for a professional game in Minnesota.

Minneapolis won the fourth game 77-69 in front of 10,512—another record-breaking crowd. Mikan poured in 28, followed Pollard with 17 and Mikkelsen with 14, as the big three scored 59 of the Lakers' 77 points. Although the Nats had a better shooting percentage, the Lakers' superior height gave them command of the boards, allowing them to take 12 more shots.

Back on their own court, the Nationals captured the fifth game of the series 83-76. Paul Seymour held Pollard to six points, and later told the press, "I hugged him and he had no place to go with Mikan clogging the middle." With Seymour's defense keeping Pollard under wraps, Mikan and Mikkelsen were the only Lakers in double figures.

The series then returned to Minneapolis for game six at the Minneapolis Auditorium before a home audience of 9,812. Three fights broke out during the game, and the first was between Pollard and Seymour. The Laker star was sending a message that he would not be "hugged" any more. With Mikan pouring in 40 and Pollard adding 16, the Lakers won by a fifteen-point margin, 110-95, to garner its third consecutive championship.

By winning all of the playoffs and the championship series, the ten Lakers split a grand total of $20,270.

Top row: Bud Grant, Tony Jaros, Swede Carlson, Dugie Martin, George Mikan, Arnie Ferrin, Coach John Kundla, Buddy Hassett. Bottom Row: Front Trainer Bob Polk, Vern Mikkleson, Bob Harrison, Herm Schaefer, Jim, General Manager Max Winter

5
THE STRING IS BROKEN

> *"...Jim Pollard was just as important (as George Mikan) to the Lakers' success. We always tried to invent strategies to beat the Lakers but never succeeded in containing Jim...He was the player we feared most at the end of the game."*
>
> – Harry Gallatin, New York Knicks

During the off-season, the Lakers added Joe Hutton, Jr. and Kevin O'Shea to their roster. Hutton had played guard for his father at Hamline University. As he grew accustomed to the competition and routines of the professional game, what impressed him most about the Lakers was the team's cohesiveness stood out. The players went out together and the Pollards or the Mikans would host parties. Once a month the owner, Ben Berger, would host the players, coaches, and their wives for dinner at Sheik's. Ben's wife Midge was a big Laker fan, had a front row seat, and never missed a game. With the long train rides and heavy schedules, Hutton said you "could count the number practices on one hand."

Hutton and the Lakers were a perfect fit. "I was at the right place at the right time. I had brought the ball up at

Dinner at Sheik's. Left to Right: George & Pat Mikan, Arilee & Jim Pollard, Marty & Gil Swenberger, *Minneapolis Tribune* sportswriter Sid Hartman, John & Marie Kundla, Ben & Midge Berger (Lakers and Sheik's owner).

Hamline and guarded the best player on the other team. The Lakers needed somebody who could come off the bench and do that." The leaders of the team, he recalled, were Mikan and Pollard. He remembered Pollard as confident and quiet. "If you made a mistake, he would never say a word to you." According to Hutton, Pollard would draw the opposing team's best defender, and they would sometimes try to intimidate the graceful forward physically. Teammate Arnie Ferrin recalled that in one game, after Jim had faked out Blackie Towery of the Baltimore Bullets several times, Towery responded "with a solid right hand that knocked Jim into the third row." After the game Pollard laughed the incident off.

The Lakers' second addition, Kevin O'Shea, was a product of San Francisco basketball, where he played at St. Ignatius High School. During the war, he played with Pollard on the Alameda Coast Guard team. An All-American at Notre Dame, O'Shea's college and professional careers were plagued by knee problems. The 1950-51 season was his only season with the Lakers.

In the summer of 1950, the NBA was reduced from seventeen to eleven teams, as organizations in Anderson, Denver, St. Louis, Sheboygan, Waterloo, and Chicago folded. Of the original BAA teams, only New York, Philadelphia, and Boston remained, and the league began to rely more than ever on teams from the small and medium-sized markets of the former NBL such as Minneapolis, Rochester, Syracuse, Fort Wayne and Tri-Cities. The Eastern Division of the shrunken league included the Philadelphia Warriors, the Boston Celtics, the New York Knickerbockers, the Syracuse Nationals, the Baltimore Bullets and the Washington Capitols, who dropped out of the league after thirty-five games. The Lakers rivals in the Western Division were the Rochester Royals, the Fort Wayne Pistons, the Indianapolis

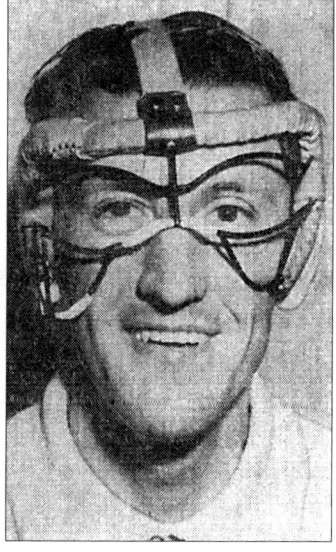

Suffering from an eye injury, Pollard takes time off to wrap presents with son Jack. With the help of a mask, Pollard returned to the line-up three weeks later. (The mask now hangs in the Naismith Basketball Hall of Fame.)

Olympians and the Tri-Cities Blackhawks.

The Lakers won the Western Division title that year with a 44-24 mark, nosing out the Rochester Royals by three games. Pollard missed fourteen games after fracturing his cheekbone in a collision with Ralph Beard of the Indianapolis Olympians on December 15. Arnie Ferrin remembered that night well, since he picked Pollard up from the hospital after the game. Pollard's eye socket was broken above and below his eye. After a very rough night, the eye socket collapsed while Pollard was shaving, and he had to return to the hospital to have it put back in place. Having seen the injury from close range, Ferrin was sure Pollard would be out for the season, but three weeks later, with a aid of plastic face mask, he was back on the floor. Mikkelsen also missed four games that year with a sprained ankle, and just as the regular season ended, Mikan suffered a hairline fracture of his ankle.

In the first round of the playoffs, the Lakers nosed out the Indianapolis Olympians 2-1. This set up a best-of-five series with the Rochester Royals, who had eliminated the Fort Wayne Pistons by the same margin. The rivalry between the two teams went back several years, and was one of the hottest in the NBA. The Lakers had a slight edge in this duel, but with Mikan playing injured, the Royals smelled victory. They were also the sentimental favorites, largely because it was thought that continued Laker dominance would not be good for the sport.

In a very unusual decision, the NBA decided to delay the opening of the finals by one day to give the injured Mikan an extra day of rest. Les Harrison, the Royals owner-coach, was justifiably upset. He became angrier when he learned that his team would have to practice at the Minneapolis Athletic Club rather than the Minneapolis Armory. Rochester had not played in the Armory for three years and George Beahon of the *Democrat Chronicle* complained that "the champions seem to want every edge."

In the opener, Mikkelsen scored 23 and Mikan came off the bench to score 22 in a narrow 76-73 Laker victory. Beahon reported that Mikan was limping noticeably, "a pathetic imitation of the real thing. He's playing on courage and instinct, but can still hit the hoop." Two nights later the Royals took the home court advantage away from the Lakers with a 70-66 win. The star of the game for the Royals was Red Holzman. Inserted in the starting lineup, Holzman responded by shooting 10 of 13 from the field and 3 of 4 from the foul line for 23 points. He also held Slater Martin to one basket. The Royals played a control game, and, according to Beahon, "with less than five minutes to go they began a very scientific freeze that protected a two-point margin down to the final buzzer." Pollard with 20 and Mikan with 18 led the Lakers.

Before the third game, Mikan, on the advice of Rochester's Jack Coleman, applied ethyl chloride to reduce the pain in his injured ankle. The Royals, however, had the momentum and stunned the Lakers 83-70, largely on the strength of a staggering 58-36 rebounding advantage. Mikan's injury was clearly hurting the Lakers in the battle for the boards, and a worried John Kundla observed: "People underestimate or don't realize the value of rebounds."

George Beahon wrote that game four was "a must game" for Rochester. The Royals did not want to fly back to Minneapolis for a fifth game. Down two games to one, the Lakers situation was more desperate. A capacity crowd of 4260 filled Edgerton Arena for the match-up and the teams did not disappoint them. When the dust settled, the Royals emerged on top 80-75, ending the Lakers streak of three championships despite 32 points from Mikan and 18 from Pollard.

Pollard and Chuck Cooper

Beahon described the game as "a bitter rock'em, sock'em ball game that kept a standing room only turnout roaring from the outset." With fifty seconds left to play, Pollard hit a hook shot to cut Rochester's lead to one point, 75-74. Then Joe McNamee, a rookie, who had only come into the game for the last two minutes, made a key tap-in after a missed free throw to ice the game. One key to Rochester's victory was that Jack Coleman limited Mikkelsen to 4 points, collecting 15 of his own. Arnie Risen led all Rochester scorers with 26.

After the game, Pollard visited the Royals dressing room to congratulate the new Western Division champs, expressing the hope that the Royals would "go all the way" and keep the title in the Division. The Lakers offered no alibis for their defeat. Injuries, they knew, were part of the game. Both teams remembered that in the 1948 finals the Royals had to play without an injured Arnie Risen.

The elimination of the Lakers was not the only news of the 1950-51 season, however. In several ways the year was a watershed for the NBA. By the season's end the league had stabilized at ten teams. Its goal was now to figure out how it could capture the imagination of the American sports fan. As part of that effort, in January 1951 the NBA held its first All-Star Game. The Lakers were represented by Mikan, Mikkelsen, and Pollard.

Of much greater significance in the long haul, the first African Americans appeared on NBA rosters during the 1950-51 season. The previous April the Boston Celtics had drafted Chuck Cooper of Duquesne University, the Washington Capitols had selected Earl Lloyd of West Virginia State College, and Ned Irish, president of the New York Knickerbockers, had purchased Nathaniel "Sweetwater" Clifton's contract from the Harlem Globetrotters.

While the introduction of African American players would have profound long-term significance for the NBA, the league received an unexpected boost when, in January 1951, New York District Attorney Frank Hogan arrested a gambler and three CCNY players for fixing college basketball games. Eventually 32 players were indicted.

Over the course of time Ned Irish had turned Madison Square Garden into a college basketball mecca, and it had subsequently become a haven for gamblers. As the press revealed the seamy underside of college basketball, the finals of the NBA season offered fans a respite from controversy. Fortunately for the NBA, the finals that year matched the Rochester Royals against the New York Knicks, and the tournament promised to supply all the drama fans had come to expect from great sporting events as well as a big-city draw.

The match-up between the Royals and the Knicks had the makings of a classic encounter—Joe Six-Pack against Donald Trump. Les Harrison had scuffled all of his life to keep basketball alive in Rochester. He was a little rough around the edges and had earned a reputation for being mildly eccentric. The Knicks' owner, Ned Irish, ran Madison Square Garden, which by 1951 had become the best known sports arena in the United States. But Irish, too, was the product of a hardscrabble upbringing. He was raised in Lake George, New York, and was only three when his father died, leaving the family in a tough spot. His mother later moved the family to Brooklyn, where Irish's entrepreneurial spirit and passion for sport connected. He started covering high school sports while attending Erasmus High School, and after earning a degree from the University of Pennsylvania, he returned to New York and found work as a sports journalist. While covering local college basketball games, Irish noticed that they were often jammed with fans clambering to make their way into very small auditoriums. Tapping this unexplored vein, Irish began to promote college basketball games. The success of this venture was sealed when, in 1934, he persuaded Madison Square Garden to let him promote college double headers. Irish exuded the confidence—some called it arrogance—and sophistication of the Big Apple.

Joe Lapchick, a legend in New York, had coached the Knicks in 1950-51 to a respectable but far from dazzling 36-30 mark. Playoff victories over Boston and Syracuse had earned the team a shot at the crown. Three of the Knicks, Vince Boryla, Dick McGuire, and Harry Gallatin, had played in the first NBA All-Star Game. Other key Knick players were Nat "Sweetwater" Clifton, Max Zaslofsky, Connie Simmons, and Ernie Vandeweghe.

Going into the first game at Rochester's Edgerton Sports Arena, the Knicks were a decided underdog. In three years the Knicks had never won a game in Rochester. The Royals mastery over the Knicks continued as they dominated the Knicks in the first two games 92-65 and 99-84. The series then moved to the 69th Regiment Armory in New York City; Madison Square Garden was already booked for another event. Visiting teams hated to play at the Armory because, as Andy "Fuzzy" Levane of the Royals observed, while "It's the best playing surface in the league…the baskets are tough—very rigid." But the Knicks could not cash in on the home court advantage and the Royals pulled ahead in the series, three to nil.

Then the series got interesting. In game four the Knicks fought off elimination with a 79-73 victory after blowing most of a 17-point lead. Returning to Rochester, the they proceeded to break the Royals' home-court hex by pulling out a thrilling 92-89 victory. Back at the 69th Regiment Armory, they knotted the series at 3-3 in front of a feverish crowd of 4500.

The seventh and deciding game was played in Rochester. It proved to be one of the great barnburners in NBA history. With the game tied at 75, Bob Davies drove for the basket, drew the foul, and made two free throws to give the Royals the lead—and the game.

The Knicks' coach, Joe Lapchick, was gracious in defeat. Of the champions, he said, "They wear the mantle well." He added the backhanded compliment that Rochester's fans "got away from their complacency. They rooted like real fans tonight." There were no rings, no parades, no championship trophy, but there was a whole lot of satisfaction. The Royals split $14,750 for winning two playoff rounds and the championship series. And a quarter-century later, in 1985, the NBA finally presented Les Harrison and the Royals with a championship trophy.

In a season filled with scandals, excitement, and NBA "firsts," one further event must be added to the list. The 1950-51 season produced the lowest scoring game in NBA history. On November 22, 1950 the Ft. Wayne Pistons, frustrated by the superior height and talent of the Minneapolis Lakers, decided that the best way to beat them was to hold the ball. Seven thousand fans at the Minneapolis Auditorium watched the Pistons edge the Lakers 19-18 on a last-second shot by Larry Foust. Maurice Podoloff, the NBA's president, was outraged, and in subsequent years the league made several short-lived attempts to speed up the game. But low-scoring, foul-plagued games remained all too common in the NBA until the 24-second shot clock was introduced in 1954.

During the summer of 1951 the Lakers were licking their wounds. Mikan and Pollard were both recovering from injuries suffered during the season, though Pollard continued to attend classes at the University of Minnesota and play semi-pro baseball for the Jordan, Minnesota, townball team. We might consider it strange that an NBA champion basketball player would involve himself in a semi-pro baseball league, but very few NBA stars of the time could make ends meet on their basketball earnings. Another eminent Midwest athlete, Bud Grant, once said, "I made more money playing [town team] baseball than I did playing for the Minneapolis Lakers ... and we won an NBA title while I was playing for them."

Jim's love of baseball went back to his childhood years on the playground. He pitched and played first base on Oakland Tech high school team, played American Legion ball, and

Jim strikes a pose while pitching for the Jordan Brewers.

during his term of service with the Alameda Coast guard, Jim would sometimes throw batting practice for the Oakland Athletics. While playing basketball for the Bittners, Jim also earned a letter in baseball at San Francisco State College, and in later life he sometimes remarked that if he had it to do over again, he would have followed baseball rather than basketball as a career.

Jim was a pitcher for the Jordan Brewers, though he could play every position on the field except catcher. In the course of six summer for the team, he maintained an impressive .371 batting average and a 30-19 W-L record on the mound. His best performance came on May 20, 1953, when, in a contest against the Prior Lake Jays, he struck out six while driving in seven runs with two homers.

Jim impressed his baseball colleagues with his skills but they were no less impressed with him as a person. Gene O'Brien, one of his opponents, recalled that he was "one of the guys, not aloof, as many of our great athletes are today." Jim's wife Arilee recalled that her husband was the only "outsider" on the Jordan team, but he made friends easily. The Jordan postmaster, Max Casey, was a close friend, as were teammates "Baldy" Hartkolf, Paul and Rollie Sundre, and Greg Busch. Hartkopf remembered, "Jim provided many thrills and fun times for the people of Jordan."

The whole town came out for Sunday ball. After the game, Geno Taddi would open up his bar, Geno's (which was usually closed on Sundays) for the players. He would then lock up and policeman would stand outside while the team relaxed. Jim was also an enthusiastic participant in the community snacks, brunches, and picnics that were an important part of a summer baseball experience.

One of the more amusing incidents in Jim's baseball career was what Hartkopf called the "longest home run in history." In one game Pollard hit a home run that landed in a box car of a train passing by the stadium's outfield. The next day the baseball was found in St. Peter, forty miles away from Jordan.

6

The Lakers Threepeat

Jim is more consistent, with exceptional brilliance becoming a more common experience.

- Charles Johnson, *Minneapolis Star*

By the time the Lakers reported to camp to prepare for the 1951-52 season, both Pollard and Mikan had recovered from their injuries and were ready for a new campaign. One of the biggest challenges facing them was to adjust to an important change in the NBA rules. In order to keep "big" men—and especially Mikan himself—from dominating the lane, the league had expanded the "key" under the basket from six to twelve feet. Because no one could stay in the key for more than three seconds, this new rule required the "big" men at center to exhibit greater speed and athleticism in playing their position.

George Mikan had plenty of talent to maintain his dominance in the center, regardless of the limits places upon his position. Meanwhile, the rule actually worked in Pollard's favor, by opening up the area around the basket, where he was adept at driving and taking creative shots from every angle. Pollard's scoring average had dropped the previous season, largely because of the broken cheekbone, and he was eager to bounce back from his injury with renewed vigor.

Prior to the 1950-51 season, the Lakers had become accustomed to the added revenue that accompanied a league championship. As the new season opened, Slater Martin reminded his teammates that the only way to cash in on that extra money was to win another championship. While the core of the Laker team had returned—Mikan, Mikkelson, Pollard, Martin and Harrison along with reserve Joe Hutton—the Laker management had fine-tuned its roster in an effort to recapture the NBA crown.

The Lakers utilized their territorial draft to take Myer "Whitey" Skoog, a gifted offensive player who had been an All-American at the University of Minnesota. Skoog was born on November 2, 1926, in Duluth, Minnesota. His father, Myer Martin Frantsen, had immigrated to the United States from Rolla, an island close to Norway, when he was fourteen years old. Myer changed his name from Frantsen to Skoog, as had other family members before him. After World War I, he married Nora Nelson and they proceeded to build a family.

Myer brought to America a love for outdoor sports, especially cross-country skiing, ski jumping, hunting and fishing which he imparted to his children. He and his wife remained immersed in Norwegian culture and Myer Jr. did not start speaking English until he was in first grade. His first grade teacher once wrote Whitey's parents a letter which said: "If you want your kid to be an American, you had better teach him how to speak English." In reality, as Whitey Skoog told me, the kids taught the parents how to speak English.

In 1936, the Skoog family moved to Brainerd, Minnesota, and by his junior year Myer Jr. was a starter on the high school basketball team. Skoog worked on a running one-handed shot reminiscent of Hank Luisetti's in the basement of the local YMCA, and in a game against Bemidji High School during his senior year, he jumped straight in the air to get off a one-hander in an act of pure improvisation. The shot didn't go in, but Whitey Skoog was on his way to developing the jump shot for which he later became famous.

After graduating from high school, Skoog enlisted in the Navy and was stationed at Green Cove Springs, Florida, not far from Jacksonville. He was the only player on the service team with no playing time at the college level: an experience he later referred to as "humbling." It was in Florida that the towheaded Myer became "Whitey."

When he got out of the service, Skoog, without a scholarship or G.I. Bill, entered the University of Minnesota. For Whitey it was a matter of loyalty to his home state. Dave MacMillan was still the basketball coach, but in the spring of 1948, he was replaced by Ozzie Cowles, who had coached successfully at Dartmouth and Michigan. Cowles, Skoog recalled, had an excellent grasp of basketball fundamentals, tolerated "no fooling around," and loved to win. Cowles taught Skoog a stutter step which he put to good use later in his career.

Four years had passed since Whitey had inadvertently taken a jump shot in high school. While he remembered the shot, it was not part of his offensive repertoire. But in a game against Drake University in December 1948 Skoog found himself penned in, with a jump shot his only option. Unlike his first effort, this time the shot went through the basket. With Cowles's blessings, Skoog decided to refine the shot, and it made him an All-American.

With Skoog adding greater depth to the backcourt, the Lakers proceeded to draft Kansas State's Lew Hitch, a 6' 8", 205-pound center. Hitch grew up in Griggsville, Illinois, a small town in the southwestern part of the state. After playing three years of high school basketball, Hitch played his first year of college basketball at Culver-Stockton, a small liberal arts college founded by the Disciples of Christ in Canton, Missouri, on the Mississippi River. After the 1947-48 season, Hitch decided that he wanted to compete at a higher level. Since he had played against Kansas State as a freshman, Hitch drove over to Manhattan, Kansas, to meet with coach Jack Gardner. An effective recruiter, Gardner sold Hitch on Kansas State. Tex Winter was Gardner's assistant coach and an excellent teacher of basketball fundamentals. Under the guidance of Gardner and Winter, Hitch improved his skills and made the All-Conference team for the Wildcats in 1951. In that year Kansas State won the Big Eight Conference championship and an invitation to the NCAA tournament along with the title. The Wildcats advanced to the finals of that tournament before losing to Kentucky, 68-58.

The third new Laker was Howie Schultz. Playing for the Lakers was a homecoming of sorts for him. He had played his high school basketball at St. Paul Central and his college ball at Hamline College under Joe Hutton. After three years with the Anderson (Indiana) Packers of the NBL, he was traded to the Ft. Wayne Pistons in 1949. Between 1943 and 1948 Schultz also played first base for the Brooklyn Dodgers, Philadelphia Phillies, and Cincinnati Reds. Schultz was 6'6" and proved to be a valuable reserve during the 1951-52 season.

With everybody healthy, the Lakers were playing well early in the season, though they seldom dominated the opposition. Widening the lane had the desired effect of cutting Mikan's scoring slightly, but Pollard and Mikkelsen became more productive. On Christmas Day 1951, Pollard's 25 points led the Lakers to a satisfying 100-93 win over the Boston Celtics. After the game Bill Carlson wrote that "Pollard was never more sparkling," and the thought crossed Pollard's

The Lakers go barnstorming. From left: Ed Mikan, Bobby Harrison, Arnie Ferrin, owner's son Bob Berger, Tony Jaros, Vern Mikkelsen, Herm Schaeffer, Swede Carlson, George Mikan, Jim Pollard, bus driver, Bud Grant. Front: referee Pat Kennedy, Buddy Hassett.

Star wrote, "Jim is more consistent, with exceptional brilliance becoming a more common occurrence." A January 4th article in the *Christian Science Monitor* carried the headline, "Jim Pollard, Team Man." The article described Pollard as a unifying force on the Lakers. When commenting on the relationship between Pollard and Mikan, the article stated that Jim had to make an adjustment, but "did it well." A box score does not tell you how the team won, but the outcome, Pollard emphasized, "is more important than individual points." On January 16th, the Laker forward scored 25 in another win against the Celtics, despite breaking a cartilage in his nose.

The 1951-52 season followed a familiar course, with the Lakers and Royals battling for the Western Division crown. But Bill Carlson cautioned Laker fans that the days when the

Pollard, Mikan, and Mikkelsen all passed the 1,000-point mark during the 1951-52 season.

team could dominate the NBA rather effortlessly were past." The rest of the league, slowly but surely, is catching up to the Lakers." When Whitey Skoog went down with a season ending injury, the Minneapolis media thought more firepower was needed. So did the Laker management. On February 24 they purchased Frank "Pep" Saul from Baltimore. Saul had spent two seasons with the Royals, but had not played much, before being sent to Baltimore. Like so many of the guards of this era, he had a deadly two-handed set shot.

As the season progressed, the Laker management worried not only about the team's performance on the court, but also about its fan base. In 1947-48 the Lakers had drawn 117,093 in 33 games for an average of 3,548. In the next two years attendance doubled, reaching an average of 7,022, but during the 1950-51 season it dropped slightly to 232,535, an average of 6,839 per game. According the owner Max Winter, the club needed to draw 240,000 to balance the books. For 1951-52 the average price of a ticket was $1.25. The Laker payroll, according to Winter, was $100,000. Salaries ranged from $4000 for rookies to $25,000 for Mikan. Promotions cost $40,000, equipment $7,500, and the rental of the auditorium ranged from $20,000 to $28,000. Over four years, Winter claimed that Lakers earned a profit of $25,000.

While there is no way of verifying these numbers, the evidence suggests that many of the NBA franchises were hurting. Rochester's seating capacity was only 4,200, and even after winning the championship Les Harrison continued to struggle financially. Baltimore and Tri-Cities were drawing less than 100,000 for a season. Maurice Podoloff highlighted the continuing challenge faced by the NBA when he said: "We still must discover the formula to set this thing afire." Yet Podoloff also noted "more than normal" progress, especially when the NBA's financial health was placed in the context of the wider sporting scene. Baseball attendance was down and the National Football League was several years away from turning the corner on the strength of television-generated revenues. But NBA basketball was the new kid on the block and it was still trying to find its niche. The fact that the Lakers were a winning team did not guarantee box office success.

The Lakers finished the season with a 40-26 record, one game behind the Royals. Among the highlights of the season was the non-league match-up on January 2, 1952, with the Harlem Globetrotters before 20,084 at the Chicago Stadium. That night the Lakers beat the Trotters for the fifth consecutive time, 84-60, and the margin of victory annoyed Saperstein, the Globetrotters' owner, so much that he terminated the rivalry. While the teams would play one more time six years later (producing another Laker victory) the rivalry had lost it meaning.

Another highlight for the Lakers came on January 20, 1952, when Mikan poured in 61 points to lead the Lakers past the Rochester Royals. Despite this scoring outburst, for the first time in his professional career, Mikan did not finish the season as the league's scoring leader. That honor went to Paul Arizin, a sharp-shooting forward with the Philadelphia Warriors who took the crown with a 25.4 average to Mikan's 23.8.

In fact, Mikan scored 400 fewer points in 1951-52 than the previous year, probably due to the expanded key. But by the last game of the season, both Pollard and Mikkelsen scored enough points to break the 1000-point plateau. Until that season no team had ever had three players score more than a thousand points, but Mikan, Pollard, and Mikkelsen did it for the Lakers, and so did Davies, Wanzer, and Risen for the Royals. On the defensive side of the ball, on February 3, Slater Martin held Davies without a basket for the first time in his professional career. The Royals star managed only one free throw as the Lakers clung to 77-75 victory. Finally for the second time, Pollard, Mikan, and Mikkelsen represented the Lakers in the NBA All-Star game.

The Lakers took the first round of the playoffs from the Indianapolis Olympians, and after the deciding game Herm Schaefer, a former Laker who had gone on to coach Indianapolis, commented: "I don't know when they've been so good."

The Olympians began their short NBA history as a Cinderella story but ended it in infamy. In 1948 and 1949, the Kentucky Wildcats had won back-to-back NCAA championships, and in 1948, five of the Wildcats also represented the United States in the Summer Olympics in London. Two of the team's biggest stars were Alex Groza, a gifted 6' 7" center, and Ralph Beard, a lightning quick guard. After their senior years Beard, Groza, and three Kentucky teammates formed the nucleus of the Indianapolis team. The players were given shares in the franchise as the NBA attempted to capitalize on their fame. Beard and Groza played in the first NBA All-Star Game. In his first two years Groza finished second to Mikan in the NBA scoring race. What looked like two Hall of Fame careers came crashing to an halt when, in October 1951, it was revealed that Groza and Beard had taken money from gamblers to control the point spread while playing for Kentucky. The NBA took quick action and banned them from the league.

After eliminating the beleaguered Olympians, Minneapolis met Rochester in a back-and-forth Western Division final. The Royals seized the opener on their home court, but the next night the Lakers pulled out an overtime win, though Mikan had fouled out with four minutes left in regulation, and both Mikkelsen and Martin were forced to ext for the same reason soon afterward. Throughout the game, the *Tribune* staff correspondent later reported, "Pollard was at his greatest—scoring, playing defense, and great on the backboards." In front of a partisan crowd, the Lakers had won a great team victory.

In game three, played in Minneapolis, the Lakers were nursing a slim 61-58 margin with seven minutes left to play, before securing a 77-67 victory. The Lakers strategy of distributing points continued as four Lakers scored in double figures led by Pollard's 22. Bill Carlson exclaimed that Pollard "chose this night for one of his greatest all around performances." The defensive star for the Lakers was Slater Martin who held Bob Davies scoreless, the first time that had happened in the Rochester's star's professional career.

The dramatic series ended the next night when Pollard tipped in a Mikan miss as time ran out to give the Lakers an 82-80 victory. After the game, an excited Pollard exclaimed, "There were a lot of dollars signs on the backboard when I went up." All five Lakers starters were in double figures with Mikkelsen and "Pep" Saul leading the way with 18 apiece. The game was tied five times in the fourth period, the last time at 80 as a result of a Joe Hutton free throw. The Lakers controlled the ball for the last two minutes and fifty-seconds before the winning basket. Oddly, Pollard's follow-up was one of his easiest shots of the series. Odie Spears, who was defending him, thought the ball was going to bounce off the front of the rim; instead, it slid off the side. "All I had to do was put it in," Pollard said later.

After the game Joe Hendrickson wrote: "The Lakers celebrated like a college team," and "staged the happiest celebration of their five-year existence. Bobby Harrison picked up *Tribune* sportswriter Sid Hartman and carried him under a shower to give the latter a thorough soaking, gabardine suit and all." Dick Cullum chose to focus on the high quality of the Minneapolis-Rochester rivalry. After five years, he noted, placing the game in historical perspective, "They've never sent a crowd away disappointed." He thought the competition between the two teams matched that of the Giants and Dodgers in baseball. "It's nice to beat the Royals, but when it's over," he concluded, "you kinda like them. They are a great team."

Jim Pollard's play earned special attention from both Hendrickson and Cullum. While Hendrickson admired the performances of all the Lakers in the Rochester series, he thought that Pollard in particular had played two nights of basketball that anyone who saw them would never forget. Nearly all of Pollard's field goals during those two games were of the sensational type, off-balance shots taken from difficult angles." Pollard, he continued, "has become the quarterback, the clutch man, the back breaker.... Right now Pollard is sinking 'em when they hurt the other guy. He's playing team ball, and who looks more secure than this dribbling antelope when the Lakers are trying to keep possession?" If Hendrickson had any criticism of Pollard, it was that "he takes daffy shots and wild chances at times. But they aren't daffy when they go in."

Dick Cullum focused on a different characteristic of Pollard's play—his consistency. During the regular season, in Cullum's view, Pollard had veered repeatedly from brilliant to indifferent. "To be frank about it," Cullum wrote, "there are times when a coach might feel justified in knotting a towel around Jim's neck and pulling hard on both ends, calling for help if necessary." This all changed with the playoffs. Then, Cullum continued: "When the money is up, Jim plays basketball for which there are no adequate words." Against the best players, when it counted the most, Pollard was in a class by himself. And what was more, Cullum concluded, Pollard had been playing on this exalted level for five years!

The New York Knicks

The Lakers were exhilarated by their victory over the Royals, but they still had to face the Knicks for the league trophy. The Knicks had finished third in the NBA's Eastern Division with a modest 37-29 record that year, but once again they had upped their game in the playoffs, eliminating the Boston Celtics and Syracuse Nationals to reach the finals. The rivalries between these three teams was extremely heated at the time, and after the third game of the semifinals between New York and Syracuse, Leonard Koppett noted that the history of the series "has been replete with arguments, fist fights, and fan trouble."

Joe Lapchick, New York's coach, was already a basketball legend. Born in Yonkers in 1900 to immigrant parents from Czechoslovakia, Lapchick left public school at the age of 14 to supplement the family's income. Joe was tall, eventually reaching six foot five inches, and gifted athletically. After playing for a variety of semi-pro teams, in the early 1920s he joined the New York Celtics, the preeminent professional team of that period. After the Celtics disbanded, Lapchick played for two years with the Cleveland Rosenblums. In 1930, he reorganized the Celtics and finished his career with them in 1936, when St. John's University named him its basketball coach. Although Lapchick had only an eighth-grade education, in those days it was common to assume that great players would make great coaches. For Lapchick, the timing could not have been better. Ned Irish, with his college double headers and National Invitational Tournament (NIT), was turning New York City into the basketball capital of the United States. Lapchick understood the limits of his education, but he was bright and worked hard to overcome them. In an extremely competitive atmosphere, Lapchick won back-to-back NIT titles in 1943 and 1944. In 1947 he left St. John's to coach the Knicks.

By the 1950s, Joe Lapchick's coaching persona was well-established. A successful basketball coach needs many talents, one of which is the ability to work with the media. Sportswriters liked Joe. He loved to dissect basketball games and share his knowledge of the game's history. Writers would follow him to one of his favorite restaurants, usually Momma Leone's, and listen as he held court. This may have been good therapy for Lapchick, who often became intensely involved emotionally during games, smoking cigarettes on the bench and throwing his water cup. The emotional wringer of basketball life took its toll and may have shortened his life. Lapchick was imperturbable off the court, and he sometimes mused on how a game had created this other personality. Since the writers liked him, they were prepared to forgive his emotional outbursts. Lapchick also took his role as a mentor to his players seriously. Though such opportunities were more plentiful during his years as a college coach, one of his Knick players, Harry Gallatin, thought of him as a father figure.

The sportswriters knew Lapchick was not an X's and O's guy, but at the professional level this was not important. Lapchick, of course, had a plan. The Knicks played a style of motion offense derived from New York City college basketball. The idea was to pass and cut and look for the open man. (Knicks fans would see the same kind of basketball again in the early 1970s when New York won two NBA titles under the leadership of Willis Reed and Walt Frazier.) But more than anything else, Lapchick worked to instill his players with the proper attitude toward competition. There was a way to compete, to respond to victory, and to handle defeat. If you mastered these, in Lapchick's words, you "could walk with kings."

The motion offense was well-suited to the personnel on the Knicks' roster, which sported a collection of talented players but no dominant star. The trigger of the offense was Dick McGuire, who had played for Lapchick at St. John's. McGuire's parents, John and Winnifred, owned McGuire's Bar on Rockaway Beach. McGuire had been a non-starter in high school, scoring a grand total of 18 points as a senior with LaSalle Academy. Nonetheless, in the fall of 1943 he was starting for Lapchick at St. John's University. McGuire won the Haggerty Award in 1944, given to the New York's best college player.

McGuire entered the Navy's V-12 program that year, and was stationed in Hanover, New Hampshire, where he proceeded to play the end of 1943-44 season with Dartmouth College, helping them to reach the NCAA finals. After playing for two armed services teams, Great Lakes and Fleet City, McGuire returned to St. John's in 1946. He was named to the All-Metropolitan team for the next three years and won the Haggerty Award again in 1949, the year the Knicks made him a territorial draft choice. By 1952, this future Hall of Famer had established himself as one of the consummate guards in the NBA. A clever passer who could run all day, McGuire made everyone around him a better player.

Vince Boryla, one of the Knicks' starting forwards, was the son of Polish immigrants. He grew up in East Chicago, Indiana, and starred at Washington High School in East Chicago, where his coach, Nelson "Doc" Irwin, taught him "more basketball than all the coaches he would subsequently play for put together." While Vince had numerous scholarship offers, there was no doubt that this son of Catholic parents would enroll at Notre Dame once it knocked on his door. In his first year at Notre Dame, 1944-45, Boryla set new season and single game scoring records. Because of the war, Boryla only played one more year for Notre Dame before the Army stationed him in Denver, Colorado, where he played two years for the Denver Nuggets, one of the powerhouse teams in AAU basketball. A two-time AAU All-American, Boryla was selected to play on the 1948 U.S. Olympic team. He finished his collegiate career in 1948-49 with the University of Denver.

Whether he was at Notre Dame, with the Denver Nuggets, or at the University of Denver, Boryla always had big games at Madison Square Garden. As a result he caught the attention of Ned Irish, who in 1949, was eager to strengthen his team. Bright and confident, Boryla was a good negotiator even at 22. He and Irish agreed upon a three-year guaranteed contract worth $49,500 paid over four years at $12,500 per year.

By 1952, it was clear that Boryla's negotiating skills were only getting sharper. He announced that he was considering retirement at the tender age of 24 to pursue business opportunities in Denver. He said, "I don't want to become a basketball bum." At 6' 5" and 212 pounds, he had been the team's high scorer in 1950-51 with a 14.9 average. He speculated that he might reconsider retirement if the money made it worth his while. At a time when all the teams traveled by train, poker was one of the ways of passing the time. Boryla was the team's captain on the floor and organized the poker games off the floor.

At the Knicks' other forward was a country boy, 6' 6" Harry "the Horse" Gallatin who weighed 210 pounds. Gallatin grew up on a farm in Wood River, Illinois, just east of St. Louis. He graduated from Roxanna High School in 1943 where he played basketball, baseball, football, and track. After a 15-month tour of duty in the Navy, Gallatin enrolled at Kirksville State College (today Northeast Missouri State University). He caught the eye of Knicks scouts Leo Gottlieb and Bud Palmer at a National Association of Intercollegiate Basketball tournament, and they drafted him in 1948. Though Gallatin still had a year of college eligibility left at the time, he already had enough credits to graduate, and he played his first game in a New York uniform on November 20, 1948. His starting salary was $4500.

Gallatin earned his nickname for his rebounding ability and durability. Besides having good hands, Gallatin had a nose for the ball. A big part of rebounding is wanting the ball, establishing position, and not being afraid to mix it up underneath the basket. Gallatin had the stitches and the statistics to go with his reputation as one of the top rebounders of his era. It eventually earned him a place in the Basketball Hall of Fame.

Completing the Knicks frontline was Nat "Sweetwater" Clifton. In 1942 Clifton established himself as one of the legends of Chicago High School basketball. On successive nights Clifton scored 45 and 24 points to lead the all-black Du Sable Panthers to the city championship. After high school Clifton played a year at Xavier University which had a pipeline to Chicago's black community. Following a stint in the army, he toured with the New York Rens and the Harlem Globertrotters. In 1950, after a contract dispute, the Globetrotters sold Clifton's contract to the Knicks. At 6'5" and 220 pounds, Clifton was a gifted athlete. He had huge hands and could easily palm two basketballs, one in each hand, simultaneously. Vince Boryla remembered "Sweets" as extremely strong, and with his unusually long arms, he played a little bigger than 6'5".

By nature a sensitive person, Clifton struggled with his role as one of the first three black players in the NBA. In his first season Clifton was very tentative, seemingly afraid of offending teammates and opponents. In his second year Clifton loosened up and averaged 10.6 points and 11.8 rebounds per game. In a game in Boston, when Bob Harris called him a "nigger," Clifton decked him, to the delight of Lapchick and his teammates. While nothing could eliminate the complications of playing in a white world, Clifton appreciated the camaraderie of being part of a team that included him in all its activities. He was a regular in all the poker games, and, as Vince Boryla remarked with a smile, "a pretty easy mark who never quite figured out when to hold them and when to fold them."

Connie Simmons, at 6' 8" and 225 pounds, was also an important piece of the Knick offense. He could play center or forward and had a deadly two-handed set shot. Simmons had never played college ball, but started his pro career at the age of 20 with the Boston Celtics; he later moved on to the Baltimore Bullets before joining the Knicks in 1949.

Max Zaslofsky was the other starting guard. He had played high school ball at Thomas Jefferson in Brooklyn. After two years in the Navy, Zaslofsky played one year at St. John's University in 1946 before signing a contract with the Chicago Stags in the BAA. At 6' 2" Zaslofsky possessed one of the best two-handed set shots in the game. He was Chicago's leading scorer and All-BAA for the four years of the franchise's existence. In the summer of 1950, when the Stags folded, the NBA had to figure out how to distribute the team's players. The owners could not agree on who should receive the two most coveted players—Max Zaslofsky and Andy Phillip. Ned Irish was especially determined to get Zaslofsky. An established star, Zaslofsky was Jewish and a New Yorker. When Irish, Eddie Gottlieb of Philadelphia, and Walter Brown of Boston dug in their heels, Maurice Podoloff decided to resolve the deadlock by throwing the names of the two players in a hat along with a player who had just been drafted, Bob Cousy. Irish pulled out Zaslofsky's name to his great satisfaction, Gottlieb got Phillip, and Brown was left with Cousy. Ironically, everybody's third choice, Cousy, would become one of basketball's greatest stars of the 1950s.

New York's sixth man was Ernie Vandeweghe, a 6' 3", 195-pound guard from Colgate. Born in Montreal, Canada, Vandeweghe grew up in Oceanside, New York, where he lettered in four sports. During four years at Colgate he scored 1377 points establishing a new scoring record at the school. Following his senior year, in which he earned All-American honors, Vandeweghe entered Columbia Medical School. Joe Lapchick convinced him that it was possible to sandwich in a pro basketball career between his medical studies. Between 1950 and 1953, Vandeweghe effectively balanced his life as a medical student with professional basketball player.

Though they boasted an impressive roster of players, the Knicks were at a disadvantage going into the finals against the Lakers. Boryla was out with a knee injury and Carl Braun, who led the Knicks in scoring between 1947 and 1950, was in the service. Lapchick was going to need help from his bench. Ray Lumpp, a 6' 1", 180-pound left-hander, helped at the guard position. Lumpp, a native New Yorker, set a scoring record while at New York University playing for Howard Cann. In 1948 NYU lost to St. Louis University in the NIT finals. When St. Louis decided against participating in the Olympic trials, NYU took its place. One result was that the U.S. Olympic Basketball Committee named Lumpp to the 1948 Olympic team that won the gold medal in London.

George Kaftan, 6' 3", was a small forward with good leaping ability. In 1947, as a sophomore, Kaftan led Holy Cross to an NCAA championship. He earned All-America honors in 1947 and 1948. Finally, the Knicks could call on Al McGuire, Dick's brother. Al had also played at St. John's University. A scrappy defender, Al McGuire had limited offensive skills. (He would make his mark in basketball at Marquette University, where he coached the Warriors to the 1977 NCAA championship.)

The Knicks were confident as the finals began, and Al Cervi, coach of the Syracuse team the Knicks had just defeated, predicted that "the Knicks won't lose a game in New York and all they have to do is take one of the games out there."

The NBA finals opened at the St. Paul Auditorium with the Lakers prevailing in overtime 83-79. Glen Gaff's lead was: "If anyone ever doubted Jim Pollard's brilliance, he should be convinced today." Pollard had a spectacular game, scoring a career high 34 points, seven of them in overtime.

In an interesting sidelight, the Knicks filed an protest after the game claiming that referee Sid Borgia had failed to see a basket made by Al McGuire near the end of the first period. Pep Saul had fouled McGuire as he drove for the basket and Borgia awarded McGuire two free throws, but the Knicks argued that a basket had also been scored. Since the game ended in a tie that forced an overtime, the Knicks thought Borgia had cost them the game. The officials were not convinced.

The next night the Lakers surrendered their home court advantage as Ray Lumpp came off the bench to score 15 and the New Yorkers won 80-72. This was the Knicks first victory in Minneapolis in thirteen attempts. How had they done it? Slater Martin put it bluntly: "We played bad basketball." Glen Gaff agreed and thought "the Lakers played one of their worst, if not their worst game in their five year history before 6,500 fans. They made every mechanical error in the book."

The two teams flew to New York where the confident Knicks had won their last 23 games. In the first game at the 69th Regiment Armory, however, the Lakers prevailed 82-77. Leonard Koppett, writing for the *New York Herald Tribune*, explained the plan was "to run the Lakers to death, win at home last night and tomorrow, play brilliant 5-man fast-break basketball that won games and wowed spectators." Louis Effrat, who covered the game for the *New York Times*, observed, "It is not often the Knicks lose at home, but when they do it's a 'beaut'." Effrat reported that with the game tied at 71 and six minutes left, "Mikan's rebounding and Pollard's passing" were the difference for the Lakers. Mikan led all Lakers with 26, and Pollard, Saul, and

Mikkelsen scored in double figures. The *Morning Tribune* reported that Pollard "played a brilliant last three periods." Lapchick was not surprised by the Laker performance and noted that "Minneapolis didn't become champs three times because they were bums or lucky."

During the game many observers took note of the fact that Ray Meyer, Mikan's coach at DePaul, was sitting on the bench beside him. In fact the Lakers had invited Meyer to the game to talk to his star pupil. Mikan had not been very productive in the first two-playoff games and the Lakers needed him at his best. The problem, as Meyer recalled, was that "George was taking shots from the top of the circle instead of being under the basket where he belonged. Well, I berated George in front of his teammates and told him to play where he belonged." Meyer's tongue-lashing obviously worked. After the game, Pollard told Meyer he had never seen anything quite like the De Paul coach's halftime tongue lashing.

Game four was another closely-fought battle and an extremely well-played game which ended in an one-point overtime victory for the Knicks in front of a capacity crowd of 5200. Connie Simmons led the Knicks scoring with 30 points, and Slater Martin kept the Lakers in the game with 32. Martin could not take too much pleasure in his scoring outburst, because, as he said, "We didn't win." After the game coach Kundla complained that the Lakers had been robbed: The officials had called Martin for carrying the ball five times, taking key baskets away from the Lakers.

The two teams returned to Minneapolis for the fifth game but a back injury kept Pollard out of the lineup. The teams were separated by a single point at halftime, but the Lakers blew out the Knicks in the third period and went on to win 102-89. Mikan and Mikkelsen each scored 32, and the effort pushed Mikan passed the 10,000 point mark for his career. Bobby Harrison filled in admirably for the injured Pollard, scoring 13.

Back in New York, and with their backs to the wall, the Knicks posted a 76-68 win to force a seventh game. Max Zaslofsky the Knicks while Simmons continued to impress with 15. Mikan had 28 points but Saul with 11 was the only other Laker in double figures.

On April 25, before 8,612 faithful Laker fans, the Lakers won their fourth championship in five years with a convincing

Slater Martin, George Mikan and Jim Pollard celebrate with Coach Kundla after the finals in New York.

82-65 victory. Mikan scored 22 and four other Lakers put up double figures as the Lakers dominated the Knicks. Pollard, his back wrapped in tape, returned to the line-up and "provided the fourth-quarter spark that gave the winners their final 17-point margin...." He scored all of his ten points in the final quarter and repeatedly broke the Knicks' press. "He broke our back," Joe Lapchick said after the game. The jubilant Lakers carried off coach Kundla on their shoulders as they celebrated their fourth championship. Afterwards they divided the post-season earnings of $14,750.

The 1951-52 season was especially satisfying for Pollard. He played 65 games, scored 1005 points for a 15.5 average, pulled down 593 rebounds, and dished out 234 assists. Fans and sportswriters throughout the league continued to be impressed with his play, and in December 1952, when a group of NBA players were asked to name the best players in the league's history, Jim Pollard came out on top (see opposite page). Joining him on the first team were Ed Macauley and Bob Cousy of the Boston Celtics, Paul Arizin and Joe Fulks of the Philadelphia Warriors, Bob Davies of the Rochester Royals, and George Mikan.

As the Lakers approached the 1952-53 season, they added Jim Holstein, a 6' 3" guard from the University of Cincinnati. Holstein grew up in Hamilton, Ohio, and played baseball, basketball, and football at Hamilton Catholic High School. In 1948 Hamilton Catholic finished second in the Ohio State Basketball Tournament. Holstein played three years of varsity ball for the Bearcats and set single season and three-year scoring records.

The Lakers continued to play a demanding exhibition season, not only before the season but during it. In December they played six exhibition games in addition to their busy

On December 16, 1952, *The Sporting News* carried an article by Jack Barry of Boston called "The Ballplayer's Ballplayer." It presented the results of a survey taken among active players who had spent at least 6 years in professional basketball. They were asked to name the most outstanding ball player they had played against. Jim was voted #1 with 33 votes, followed by George Mikan and Ed McCauley with 27 votes apiece. Bob Cousy and Joe Fulks filled out the "starting" five. Spares: Bob Davies and Paul Arizin. 2nd team: Max Zaslofsky, Dolph Schayes, Andy Phillip, Bob Wanzer, Bob Ferrick. Honorable Mention: Vern Mikkelsen, Ralph Beard, Dick McGuire, Bones Mckinney, John Mahnken, Fred Scolari, Red Rocha, Alex Groza, Johnny Logan and Jack Nichols.

NBA schedule. On New Year's Eve, management instructed the players not to make any plans; the team had planned a "Celebrate New Years Eve with the Lakers" promotion for that night. The rationale offered by management was that "we must promote more than ever. Our crowds are down considerably…." Management told the players that without the exhibition games, the team would go out of business. The regular season was grueling enough and the players were not excited about traveling to small towns in Iowa, Minnesota, and Wisconsin to play meaningless games, but the management said: "It's up to you to put out 100 percent at all times." The club was particularly upset about the team's effort in one exhibition game and warned the players that they weren't going to stand for any such performance again. Management also tried to monitor player conduct. There were fines for "drinking whiskey in a bar or night club during the season" or "smoking within six blocks of any floor we play on."

During the season the Lakers played extremely well and finished with a league-best 48-22 record. In the first round of the playoffs they eliminated the Indianapolis Olympians once again 2-0, which put $3,000 into their post-season pot. Their next challenge was the Fort Wayne Pistons, one of the storied professional franchises.

Fort Wayne's roots in professional basketball could be traced back to 1941-42 when it joined the National Basketball League. The owner of the team was Fred Zollner, whose father, Theodore, founded Zollner Machine Works, a company that had grown dramatically during World War II. Like many large corporations, the Zollner Machine Works developed an athletic program to provide recreation for its employees. In 1939, Fred Zollner hired Carl Bennett to direct the athletic program. Bennett had been an outstanding softball player but also had basketball experience. He would

The 1952-53 Lakers. Dugie Martin, Joey Hutton, Pep Saul, Bobby Harrison, Jim, Howie Schultz, Vern Mikkelsen, Lew Hitch, George Mikan.

go on to coach Piston softball and basketball teams. He also represented the Pistons on the NBA's Board of Governors.

For most of its history, the Pistons had played in the North Side High School Gym, but in 1951 the team moved into the War Memorial, a more spacious facility. The Pistons had knocked out Rochester in the first round of the playoffs. They had size with centers Larry Foust and Charlie Share and forwards Don Meineke and Fred Schaus. Fred Scolari, Andy Phillip, and Frank Brian were veteran guards who had won all-NBA honors.

But with Mikan and Pollard providing the scoring punch, the Lakers won the first two games in Minneapolis 83-73 and 87-75. The Pistons fought back in Fort Wayne, winning narrowly 98-95 and 85-82. The teams returned to the Minneapolis Armory for the deciding game, where, on the strength of magnificent defense, the Lakers survived the Piston challenge, 74-58. Slater Martin tied Mikan for scoring honors that night with 18 and the fiery Texan held Fred Scolari to 5. By the end of the game, the Lakers were a battered bunch. Martin nursed a sore rib, Mikan said that he "hurt all over," and Pollard's weight had dipped to 181 pounds. Max Winter declared that he had never enjoyed a win more. Scolari paid the Lakers the ultimate tribute when he said: "The Lakers still are the toughest key-game team in basketball."

The 1953 finals were a repeat of the 1952 Laker-Knicks match-up. The Knicks, who had won their division, eliminated Baltimore and Boston to make the finals. As the contest got underway they appeared to be the stronger team. Vince Boryla had recovered from a knee injury and was starting at one forward. Carl Braun had also returned to the lineup following two years in the service. Braun had starred in baseball, basketball, and soccer at Garden City High School on Long Island. As a freshman at Colgate he set a new season scoring record. In 1947, Braun signed to pitch for Newark in the Yankee's organization. In the same year, the NBA passed a rule allowing a team to draft a player who had signed a professional contract in another sport. The Knicks drafted Braun who began his career with the New Yorkers in 1947. For the next three years, he was New York's leading scorer. In 1952 he helped Fort Bragg capture the Third Army playoffs and was the tournament MVP. Knicks veterans Harry Gallatin, "Sweetwater" Clifton, Dick and Al McGuire, and Ernie Vandeweghe completed the roster of starters and reliable subs.

Both teams had experienced great success during the regular season, but the Lakers had one advantage in the playoffs—the home court advantage. The Knicks didn't like playing in Minneapolis, and with good reason—they had won there only once in the previous four seasons. But despite the odds, they surprised the experts when they beat the Lakers 96-88 at the Minneapolis Armory in the first game of the series. According to Leonard Koppett, near the end of the third period the "Knicks finally unleashed their murderous fast break" and had reduced the deficit from 10 points to one point by the end of the quarter. Sparked by Ernie Vandeweghe, who finished with 17, the Knicks outscored the Lakers by nine points in the final frame to preserve the win.

Koppett also observed, as an aside, that the Laker fans were good natured and "the hostility and bitterness that marked New York's previous series with Boston was completely absent." He had experienced a healthy dose of "Minnesota Nice."

With a victory under their belts in Minneapolis and three games scheduled for the 69th Regiment Armory in New York City, the Knicks were clearly in the driver's seat, and the following night they came a hair's breadth from cementing the position, overcoming a seventeen-point halftime deficit to grab a 65-64 lead in the fourth period. In the last nine minutes neither team scored a basket and the Lakers won the game at the free throw line, 73-71.

Although the loss was a disappointment, the Knicks were well aware that the Lakers had played seven games in the last ten days, and according to Koppett, their strategy during the three upcoming games in New York would be to run their opponents ragged and reduce them to ineffectiveness. They knew it would be necessary in any case to "break even" on the boards and contain Mikan. While some in the New York media were already crowning the Knicks champions, Koppett warned, "No one is taking anything for granted."

In the first game at the 69th Regiment Armory, Governor Tom Dewey and 5,100 Knicks fans saw their team fall 90-75. The Lakers took a 40-39 lead at the beginning of the

Celebrating another championship at the Copacabana in New York City.

third period, kept their momentum going, and the Knicks never got closer than five for the rest of the game. Mikan's 20 and Pollard's 19 led the Lakers. Pulling no punches, Koppett wrote that the Lakers "thoroughly whipped the Knicks" who "put on their worst performance since the playoffs began, doing everything wrong." By contrast the Lakers played "perhaps their best ball."

A standing-room-only crowd packed the auditorium for the next encounter, and it was a tense and closely-fought encounter. Mikan topped all scorers with 27 but fouled out with four minutes to play. Deane McGowen of the *New York Times* observed that "with Pollard and Mikkelsen still controlling the boards, Mikan's absence didn't aid the New Yorker's much." Mikkelsen also added 11 and Pollard 10 points. Tied at 65 with two minutes to play, lay-ups by Jim Holstein and Whitey Skoog gave the Lakers some breathing room. Skoog scored the clinching basket of the 71-69 Laker victory when he tipped in a missed shot by Pollard. The Lakers now held a 3-1 lead.

The momentum had shifted and now the Knicks, according to the *New York Times,* "appeared tired and at times played listlessly." But in game five, with the help of their fans, who stomped their feet and booed on every Laker free throw, the Knicks regained their energy. But despite New York's effort, six Lakers scored in double figures, led by Pollard's 17, to give the them their fifth championship, 91-84. At one point the Lakers were up by 20 points, but the Knicks closed the gap to one point 85-84 with 90 seconds left to play. The game's last six points belonged to the Lakers.

The finals generated an abundance of analysis. As usual, coach Joe Lapchick was gracious in defeat. "We had the guts" but "they had the class," he said. He was especially impressed by the Laker defense. "I never thought that ball handling would be our weakest point. We played like schoolyard kids." Lapchick thought the players "got too high when they won out there. They yelled 'We won't be back in Minneapolis;' they were going to wrap it up at the Armory." Years later Vern Mikkelsen remembered that as he walked off the court after the second game, "Sweatwater" Clifton said: "Hey Mik, We won't be back here again." When Mikkelsen got to New York the local media predicted that the series would not return to Minneapolis. As it turned out, Mikkelsen observed "they were right. It didn't."

In the eyes of many, their sixth championship was Minneapolis's finest. One key to the victory was the play of the bench. Skoog, who had played sparingly in the first two games in Minneapolis, gave the Lakers a big lift in games three and four. Holstein was a perfect 5 for 5 from the floor in game five. Mikan, Mikkelsen, and Pollard were models of consistency. Slater Martin and Pep Saul were steady at the guard positions. Though the league was still in its infancy, no team had ever before won a NBA title in just five games.

After sewing up the title, a jubilant group of Lakers—both players and management—celebrated their achievement at New York's Copacabana.

For their efforts the Lakers would split $16,500. When the Lakers returned to Minneapolis the Sports and Attractions Committee of the Chamber of Commerce fêted the Lakers at a luncheon at the Radisson Hotel. Perhaps Lou Miller of the *New York World and Telegram* summed up the season best: "The Lakers proved themselves the Yankees of the basketball world."

THE LAST CHAMPIONSHIP SEASON

As the Lakers prepared for the 1953-54 season, the most important addition to their roster was Clyde Lovellette, a 6' 9", 240-pound center. Lovellette had been an All-American at the University of Kansas. In his senior year he led the nation in scoring and also led KU to a NCAA championship. That year he also picked up a gold medal as a member of the U.S.'s Olympic Basketball team. The Lakers drafted him in 1952 but Lovellette chose to played the 1952-53 season for the Phillips Petroleum Company. At that point he signed with the Lakers, whose plan was to groom him as a successor to George Mikan.

With the acquisition of Lovellette, Howie Schultz retired and Lew Hitch was sent to Milwaukee. Dick Schnittker, who had played his college ball at Ohio State, joined the Lakers during the 1953 playoffs; 1953-54 would be his first full season with the team.

That year the Lakers won the Western Division with a 46-26 record. The team statistics reflected a familiar pattern. Mikan was the leading scorer with Pollard second followed by Mikkelsen. Pollard led the team in minutes played and was second in assists. Slater Martin was second in minutes played and first in assists. One of the key changes was that Whitey Skoog doubled his minutes played and divided time with Pep Saul at the off-guard position. Late in the season, in a move that was both bizarre and comical, the Lakers sent Bob Harrison to Milwaukee. Harrison's minutes were down, but in a game against Rochester, he led the Lakers to a come-from-behind victory. When the jubilant Harrison entered the locker room, Kundla pulled him aside and told him that he was going to Milwaukee. Harrison was dumbfounded. He later learned that after the game his wife had confronted Max Winter and told him that her husband had just proven why he should be playing more. Winter did not take kindly to the advice or the manner in which it was given, so that Harrison's career with the Lakers came to an abrupt end.

In what would become a tradition in January, the NBA took a recess from its regular schedule for its fourth All-Star game. For the first time the game was played at Madison Square Garden. On January 21, before 16,487 fans, the All-Stars put on quite a show. In a nip-and-tuck game, George Mikan sunk two free throws with one second on the clock to tie the game at 84 and send it into overtime. Jim Pollard led all scorers with 23 and the press initially named him the game's MVP. In the overtime, however, Bob Cousy caught fire and scored 14 points to give the East a 98-93 victory. After Cousy's display, the writers reconsidered their vote and made Cousy the MVP.

In 1954, the NBA abandoned a conventional playoffs system for a complicated round robin format. Bill Reddy, sports columnist for the Syracuse *Post-Standard*, wrote "When sillier playoffs are devised the National Basketball Association will think them up." In 1954, there were nine teams in the NBA and only three were eliminated from the playoffs after playing 72 games. In the round robin, each team played the other twice. The team with the worst record was eliminated. The two remaining teams would play a three game series to determine the NBA finalists. Although the Lakers had won their division, they had lost eight of their last thirteen games. Conversely, the Rochester Royals won thirteen of their last sixteen games. John Kundla said: "We weren't playing as a team." Joe Hendrickson reported that the team had three meetings to hash out their differences. Whatever the problems, the Lakers fixed them.

In their first round robin game, the Lakers overwhelmed Rochester, 109-88. The Lakers took a 63-38 halftime lead and coasted to victory. John Kundla thought "that was the greatest half we've played in all these years." Slater Martin was high man with 24, but six other Lakers were in double figures. No attendance figure were given, but Glen Gaff reported that the crowd was slim.

The next night, the Lakers played in Fort Wayne and topped the Pistons 90-85. Minneapolis caught a break when Fort Wayne's sensational rookie, George Yardley, left the game with the flu. Yardley was a Stanford star who had excelled in AAU basketball in the early 1950s. In 1958, he would be the first NBA player to score 2000 points. Two nights later, with Yardley still unable to play, the Lakers polished off the Pistons 78-73. Mikan had 21 and Pollard 20 to lead the Lakers. A mere 2,605 fans turned out for the game.

The loss eliminated the Pistons and left the Lakers and Royals to fight it out for the Western Division Playoffs championship. Though the turnout was once again disappointing—a mere 2,469 paid to see the game—the Lakers cruised by the Royals 89-76. Pollard had a sensational game. One reporter wrote that, "He did some things on the floor last night that one would call impossible if one didn't see them." At one point Pollard hit "three clutch baskets that were out of this world." The Royals knotted up the series in Rochester when Jack Coleman scored at the end of the game to give the Royals a 74-73 victory, but the Lakers, playing before 5,268 at the Minneapolis Auditorium, earned a spot in the finals by beating the Royals, 82-72.

The frustrated Royals did not take defeat graciously. After the game Les Harrison and some of his players surrounded Art Heff, one of the officials, verbally assaulted him, and impeded his path to the dressing room. Maurice Podoloff, the NBA's president, fined Harrison $500 for his antics.

Compared to the Eastern Division playoffs, the Western Division had been a tame affair. The New York Knicks had won the Eastern Division but failed to win a game in the round robin. Frustrated by his team's performance, Ned Irish, the president of the Knicks, directed his anger at the playoff system. Irish declared: "We were against it from the outset and next time we will positively not stand for it. Nobody, including the players, knew what it was about."

With New York on the sidelines, the Boston Celtics and the Syracuse Nationals faced off for the right to meet the Lakers. The Celtics, coached by Red Auerbach, were blessed with great guards. Bob Cousy directed the offense. He had great ball-handling skills and was a clutch shooter, and was already on his way to becoming a basketball legend. Born in Manhattan in 1928 to French immigrants, Cousy was an only child. His father, who drove a cab for a living, worked long hours and had little contact with his son. Like Jim Pollard, John Kundla, and so many of the athletes discussed in this book, athletics was the vehicle that took Cousy out of a working class neighborhood to a life one could only dream of living.

In the fall of 1946, Cousy was one of several New York

City players recruited by Doggie Julian to play at Holy Cross. As a freshman, though he came off the bench, Cousy was the third leading scorer on Holy Cross's 1947 NCAA championship team. The following three years he was an All-American.

Cousy's running-mate at guard was Bill Sharman. A native of California, Sharman played at the University of Southern California. Before completing his college eligibility, Sharman signed a professional baseball contract and had a cup-of-coffee with the Brooklyn Dodgers. His professional basketball career began with the Washington Capitals in 1950, but in 1951 he wound up with the Celtics. A fierce competitor with an outstanding shooting touch, Sharman was the perfect "shooting guard"—though the term was not widely used in the 1950s. The Celtics third star was its center "Easy" Ed Macauley, a two-time All-American at Saint Louis University. He was an excellent shooter and scorer at 6' 8" and 200 pounds, though he lacked the size and strength to handle the bigger centers in the league.

In 1954 the Syracuse Nationals still had the core of players who had taken them to the 1950 finals: Dolph Schayes, Billy Gabor, and Paul Seymour. By 1954 the Nats had added George King, a deadly shooter who had set small college scoring records at Morris Harvey; Wally Osterkorn, a forward from the University of Illinois; and Earl Lloyd, who, after two years in the service, was picked up by the Nats. The hard-driving Al Cervi had retired from his playing duties and was now a full-time bench coach. Syracuse had won all of their round robin games, including a 96-95 win over the Celtics. But a cloud hovered around the franchise, since it had drawn only 106,000 for the season and reportedly had lost $35,000. There were rumors that Danny Biasone had turned down $150,000 to move the team to Chicago.

Syracuse went into the Boston series short-handed—Earl Lloyd had fractured his hand against the Knicks. Nonetheless, the Nats took the first two games against Boston to win the Eastern Division playoffs.

There had been a lot of hand-wringing over fights during NBA games, and the second Boston-Syracuse game produced one of the most virulent. *The Post Standard*'s Jack Andrews wrote: "The biggest riot of the year took place after three minutes of play in the third quarter when Bob Harris smacked Dolph Schayes to the floor, cutting his eyes and injuring his right wrist in the melee." It took 25 minutes to clear the floor. Oddly, the Nats were down 53-47 when the fight broke out. Without Schayes, Syracuse wound up on top 83-76. Al Cervi described the win as the "greatest thing I've ever seen in my life." Danny Biasone chimed in: "I'll never forget this. We turned the Celtics into chokers. We've got more moxie than all the other clubs put together." The brawl was not an aberration. Hard fouls and physical intimidation were part of the game, with roots going back all the way to the 1920s.

When the NBA finals opened in Minneapolis, the Lakers faced a battered Syracuse team. Schayes had a broken wrist, Seymour a badly sprained thumb, Lloyd a fractured hand. Despite these advantages, the Lakers found themselves in a real struggle. Normally a running team, the Nats played deliberately in the first game, and with six minutes to play they were only down by four, but at that point the Lakers went on a scoring run to finish on top 79-68. Cervi thought "We played it just about right." Glen Gaff of the *Morning Tribune* agreed and wrote that the Lakers appeared "nervous and fumble-fingered." The key to the Laker victory was the play of Clyde Lovellette, who was high for the Lakers with 16. Paul Seymour limited Pollard to 4 points. The Laker captain explained: "He just played good position on me and didn't let me get any shots off. He's tough anytime."

While a disappointing 4,579 watched the first game, 6,277 arrived at the Minneapolis auditorium for game two. Cervi employed the same strategy and this time it worked. With time running out and the game tied at 60, Paul Seymour hit a long shot from around the mid-court line to give the Nats the upset victory. The game was televised nationally and marked the first playoff defeat for the Lakers on the Auditorium floor. For Syracuse, the victory was marred by an injury to George King's left wrist. At this point four of Syracuse's five starters were hampered by injuries.

The Lakers took advantage of Syracuse's misfortune by thumping the Nats in game three at Syracuse's War Memorial Stadium 81-67 before a record crowd of 8,719. Mikan scored 30, Mikkelsen 14, and Pollard chipped in with 8 points and 13 rebounds. Four nights later, the pesky Nats evened the series by pulling away from the Lakers in the fourth period to win 80-69. Paul Seymour scored 25 points to lead all scorers. More encouraging for the Nats was that Dolph Schayes, who had played sparingly in the first three games, scored 10 points and clocked 25 minutes.

In game five, the Lakers bounced back and, led by Vern Mikkelsen's 21 points, topped the Nats 84-73. Five other Lakers scored in double figures. The Lakers pulled down 65 rebounds to 31 for the Nats.

When the Lakers returned to Minneapolis, Cervi successfully persuaded the Lakers to widen the auditorium floor to the regulation fifty feet. Max Winter said: "Cervi beefed so much that we decided to satisfy him and everyone else that has complained about it." If the width of the floor changed, Cervi's strategy did not. Playing at a slow tempo, Syracuse kept the game close. With two and one-half minutes left to play, Pollard hit two free throws to tie the game at 63. The Nats froze the ball until the ten second mark, at which point Cervi called time out. On a hunch, Cervi inserted 6' 11" Jim Neal, a rookie, who proceeded to sink a 20-foot shot, his first of the game, to give the Nats the victory. Maurice Podoloff, the NBA's president, exclaimed: "I don't believe it, but I saw it. Win or lose tomorrow night, Syracuse is the greatest story in sports history."

The following night, led by Pollard's 21 points, the Lakers ended the Nats bid to unseat the champions, 87-80. Paul Seymour, who had harassed Pollard for the entire series, joked: "I knew Pollard would get mad at me one of these days and kill me." John Kundla chimed in: "Didn't that Jim Pollard play a game." Al Cervi agreed: "Pollard definitely was the man who beat us. He was great. I've always said that."

Surrounded by the press after the game Pollard laughed: "A man will do anything to get a good five months rest won't he?" In a more serious vein he observed: "Finally everybody was 'up' for this one."

Jim is running out of space in his new trophy case.

The Lakers had won their third straight championship, and their sixth in seven years. Each of the players and coach Kundla got $1,590.91 as their share of the playoff pot. Bobby Harrison received a half share. The following afternoon, 400 people paid two dollars apiece to celebrate the Minneapolis's achievements. Maurice Podoloff may have been correct when he told the gathering that "the Lakers have been the greatest contributing factor to the history of the NBA." And it would be hard to quibble at the time with his claim that the Lakers were "the greatest team in the history of basketball." In the midst of all the celebrating, few in Minneapolis could have predicted that the Lakers had delivered the last NBA championship to that city.

On the other hand, although the championship had ultimately eluded them, the valiant effort put up by the Syracuse team during their playoff run energized the franchise. The Nats had only drawn 106,000 during the season and rumors of an imminent sale swirled around the team, but their gutsy play finally captured the attention of local fans, and seizing the moment, owner Biasone announced that the franchise was putting up $200,000 of stock in the club for sale. A few days after the final game with the Lakers, eager buyers had snatched up half of it.

After the season finale, the Lakers once again started looking ahead to their off-season activities and jobs. Jim Pollard would play baseball for Jordan, Slater Martin returned to Houston, and George Mikan expected to practice law. During the euphoria following the championship, Mikan said he would play "as long as they pay me," but during the summer he began to reconsider his future. Citing the responsibilities of family life and the desire to practice law, Mikan announced his retirement on September 24 at the age of 29. Less than two weeks later, the Lakers named him the club's new general manager, and Max Winter announced that he would focus his energies on Minneapolis's effort to get a professional football team.

Jim Pollard was also thinking about his post-NBA future. In March of 1954 Bob Burnett resigned as Stanford's

Jim and Arilee enjoy some fishing during the off-season with John Kundla and his sons.

basketball coach. Pollard and Howie Dallmar, teammates on Stanford's 1942 NCAA champions, immediately surfaced as candidates for the position. Pollard was very interested in the position, and he met with Al Masters, Stanford's athletic director, to discuss the situation. Dallmar had the better resume, however, having not only played for the Philadelphia Warriors in the BAA but coached the University of Pennsylvania basketball team to an impressive 105-51 record. In the end Stanford chose Dallmar, who directed its basketball team for the next 21 seasons.

Everett Dean, who had coached both players, offered Pollard both encouragement and perspective, reminded him that the salary difference was considerable between what Stanford could offer and what the Lakers were paying him. Besides, he added, "you will not want for a college job when you drop out of pro ball." Dean thought: "Howie's case is different—he doesn't sacrifice any salary and he leaves one headache to take up another!" Dean reminded Jim that "when the time comes to look for that college job you may count on me for recommendations."

Jim with Commissioner Maurice Podoloff

When Maurice Podoloff sent Jim a $100 check for being named to the alternate All-Star team, he also offered encouragement. Podoloff wrote: "When I heard that you were to become a coach I was a little distressed, although I did hope that if you wanted to be one your desire should be satisfied. There are many who share my opinion that you are one of the 'greats' in the game and although I wish you every success in any line you choose for yourself, I know that when your playing days cease, this will constitute a loss to me and many others."

7
"The Transition Game"

Many basketball players are great with the ball but without the ball they are inept. Jim's ability with or without the ball was one of his greatest attributes that made him a Basketball Hall of Famer.

– Coach John Kundla

With the coaching door closed for the time being, Pollard prepared for another season with the Lakers. And it proved to be another watershed year, for in 1954 the league introduced the 24-second shot clock to speed up the game. Stalling had become a popular strategy, though the fans hated it, and the idea of stipulating a specific amount of time to take a shot had been discussed for several years. Syracuse's Danny Biasone is credited with determining how much time should be allowed. According to Biasone, "I looked at the box scores from the games I enjoyed, games where they didn't screw around and stall. I noticed each team took about 60 shots. That meant 120 shots per game. So I took 48 minutes—2,880 seconds—and divided that by 120 shots. The result was 24 seconds per shot."

Pollard was skeptical about the idea at first, concerned that it wouldn't give teams enough time to set up plays. (Of course, he himself was very effective at stalling when the Lakers chose to take time off the clock, and the clock eliminated this tactic.)

A second rule change gave a team an extra free throw when its opponent committed its seventh foul in a period. This was designed to prevent a team from purposely fouling in order to limit its opponent to one point rather than two. Another rule change stated that a defensive player who was fouled would not get a foul shot; his team would simply get possession of the ball. Finally any defensive foul in the back court would give the offensive player two foul shots. In the aggregate, these changes achieved the desired effect: Scoring increased and the game became more entertaining.

As important in the short term as these rule changes, the NBA also avoided a potential gambling scandal when, on March 24, 1954, Maurice Podoloff expelled Jack Molinas of the Fort Wayne Pistons from the NBA, invoking a clause in the standard contract that gave the NBA president the power to expel any player "who directly or indirectly bets money or anything of value on the outcome of any game played for any National Basketball Association Club." Molinas was a product of the Bronx, and by his teenage years he had developed a passion for basketball, an addiction to gambling, and a talent for lying. A gifted offensive player at 6' 6", Molinas starred at Columbia University, was drafted by the Pistons, and by the start of the 1953-54 season had worked himself into the team's starting lineup. But when it came to light that he had been placing bets on Pistons games with an acquaintance in New York, he was finished in the NBA.

Jim Pollard's last season in the NBA began on September 27, 1954, at the Lakers training camp on the campus of Hamline University. The challenge coach John Kundla faced that year was to devise a new offensive approach now that their towering center, George Mikan, was no longer part of the team. He hoped that Clyde Lovellette would ease the transition. The Lakers had traded traded Pep Saul to Milwaukee for Don Sunderlage during the off-season, and this also gave them new options. The only rookie to start and finish the season was Ed Kalafat, a husky football and basketball star from the University of Minnesota.

The Lakers played well in the exhibition season, but, for the first time in its history, it lost the game played annually between the College All-Stars and the previous season's NBA's champion. The collegians, led by Cliff Hagan, Bob Pettit, and Frank Ramsay, squeezed past the Lakers in overtime, 93-90, before 15,321 at the Chicago Stadium.

As the season progressed the Lakers struggled to stay above .500. On December 5, Pollard injured his leg in a game against the Milwaukee Hawks and missed nine games. As the new year opened, the Lakers were 16 and 15 and trailed the improved Fort Wayne Pistons by six games, and they face a grueling mid-January schedule, with 13 games in 15 days. The Lakers were also struggling at the gate, though when they beat the Philadelphia Warriors on January 16, Bill Carlson wrote that "a more pleasing crowd of 5,389" viewed the game. He noted that this was the second time in three games that attendance had topped 5,000. Charlie Johnson of the *Minneapolis Star* suggested that part of the problem might rest with management's decision to televise Sunday home games. Whatever the explanation, generating attendance at Laker games had become a problem.

The Lakers got a chance to rest when the NBA took a break for the All-Star game. On January 18, 1955, Jim Pollard played in his fourth and last NBA All-Star game. He was joined that day by Vern Mikkelsen and Slater Martin.

The Western All Star team of January 1955. Back: Jack Coleman, Vern Mikkelsen, injured Arnie Risen, Larry Foust, Bob Pettit, Jim Pollard. Front: Coach Charlie Eckman, Andy Phillip, Bobby Wanzer, Dugie Martin, Frank Selvy, George Yardley

Before 13,148 at Madison Square Garden, the East beat the West 100-91. Pollard with 17 and Mikkelsen with 16 led the West's scorers.

During the break, the players formed a Players Association "to work for the betterment of basketball to the mutual benefit of owners and players." The Western Division teams selected Jim Pollard as their representative. The Eastern Division clubs elected Bob Cousy to represent them. Cousy was the driving force behind what would become a successful union. In the 1954 off-season, he corresponded with team leaders including Pollard—men that Cousy felt would not be intimidated by management. The Celtic star had no union experience or radical agenda, but he was convinced that the players had a stake in the NBA's success and some legitimate grievances, the most glaring of which was the schedule, with its compulsory exhibition games. The Lakers were particularly guilty of over-scheduling exhibition games. The NBA was on notice that sooner or later, the dynamics of the league was going to change.

After the All-Star break the Lakers first five games illustrated the zaniness of its schedule. They played five consecutive games against the Milwaukee Hawks, three in Louisiana, one in Minneapolis, and another in Huron, South Dakota. The NBA scheduled three games in Louisiana because rookie Bob Pettit, a Louisiana State University star, was in Milwaukee's lineup.

More than five thousand fans showed up at one of these encounters, and after the game Peter Finney of *New Orleans States* remarked that the event had exemplified the differences between college and professional basketball, which in his view were "two different sports." Finney suggested that the pros place the emphasis on satisfying the public's thirst for spectacular action, which required keeping nitpicking officials in the background. He felt that during the game Pettit, Louisiana's rookie sensation, "was in kindergarten—lost in a welter of educated goons who can toss elbows, knees and shoulders with bruising regularity, then look humbly at the officials when a foul is called." Lovellette was the star of the game with 37 points, but Pollard, Mikkelsen, and Martin also impressed Finney. "There's no wasted motion with these guys," he observed. Although Pettit scored 16 points, Finney believed that the rookie's basketball education was just beginning. He recommended that Pettit "keep watching Pollard and Martin, and pretty soon he'll be ready for graduation too." Pettit studied well. In 1958 he led the St. Louis Hawks to an NBA title and eventually compiled a record that earned him a place in the Basketball Hall of Fame.

After the swing down South, the Lakers settled down,

and they competed the season with a 40-32 record—good enough for a second place finish in the Western Division. At the end of the season, the Lakers reacquired Lew Hitch. In fact, when Hitch was sent to Milwaukee in 1953, it had merely been a loan. The Lakers could afford to give up Hitch when Lovellette joined the team in 1953, but after

Mikan retired, they needed another big man so they called in their loan.

In the 1955 playoffs, Minneapolis and Rochester faced off for the last time in post-season play. The Royals had suffered through their first losing season in the franchise's history, 29-43. Nonetheless, the two old rivals gave their fans a good show. In the opener, before 4,841 the Lakers prevailed 82-78, and Augie Karch, who covered basketball for the *Minneapolis Morning Tribune*, described Pollard as "the rebounding genius who kept the Lakers in the game" with 16 rebounds. In game two in Rochester, the Royals prevailed 94-92, but a few days later the Lakers returned the favor on their home court to earn a place in the Western Division finals. Up by one at the half, the Lakers outscored the Royals 35-18 in the third period, and Pollard once again demonstrated his ability to get up for big games by scoring a season high 26 to go along with 6 assists and 13 rebounds. Lew Hitch broke his individual scoring record with 23 and Vern Mikkelsen added 22. The game was the last for Bobby Davies, Rochester's great star, and for coach Les Harrison.

In the Western Division finals, the Lakers met the Ft. Wayne Pistons, who had finished ahead of the Lakers by three games during the regular season. Three Piston stars—Larry Foust, Andy Phillip, and George Yardley—had been selected for the All-Star game that year. Mel Hutchins, an athletic swingman from Brigham Young University, and Bob "Hooks" Houbregs, an All-American center from the University of Washington, filled out the starting five.

Unfortunately for the Lakers, the Division finals opened in Fort Wayne one day after the day after their victory over the Royals. Taking advantage of Laker fatigue, the Pistons won the game easily, 96-79. Two days later the Lakers took the Pistons into overtime, but the Pistons emerged with the win.

In game three in Minneapolis, the Lakers turned the tables on the Pistons and won in overtime, 99-91. Whitey Skoog sent the game into overtime and led all Lakers with 24. Martin's 17, Pollard's 16, and Lovellette's 14 provided the additional fire power. Augie Karch noted that "Jim Pollard came through with five sensational shots in the last seventeen minutes." The only sour note was that a mere 4,512 watched the game. The next night, the Pistons grabbed the Western Division title 105-96. In his last game in professional basketball, Jim Pollard scored 19 points.

Injuries had marred Pollard's last season. He missed 9 games and his minutes played were down significantly. Since 1952, when the NBA began to keep this statistic, Pollard had never played less than 2400 minutes, but in In 1954-55 he logged only 1,960—the lowest of the five starters, while averaging 10.6 points per game, his lowest in eight years as a Laker.

In April 1955, Pollard announced that he had accepted a three-year contract worth $8,500 annually to coach basketball at La Salle College in Philadelphia. At that time La Salle had an enrollment of 1500 men, and its basketball program had enjoyed great success in its previous two years under coach Ken Loeffler. In 1954 the Explorers had defeated Bradley to win the NCAA title, and the next year they lost to San Francisco in the NCAA finals. After the 1955 NCAA tournament, Loeffler resigned to take the head coaching position at Texas A&M. Loeffler was a great fan of Pollard's. One standout on the 1954-55 team, Tom Gola, recalled that his coach "always said to us and anyone who listened that his ideal team was five Jim Pollards who could move the ball, score, and play defense."

Today it's hard to imagine a professional player, without

"The Transition Game"

Packing up to go to first coaching job in LaSalle College in Philadephia: Jim and Arilee with Jeanne, Jack and Jeff.

coaching experience, being given the opportunity (and responsibility) of coaching a Division One college basketball team. In the 1950s this was still possible. Pollard had always wanted to coach and had not prepared himself for another vocation. He was at the critical moment in any superior athlete's life, when circumstances require him to leave center stage. Having reached this point, Pollard admitted, "I don't know if I'll be a good coach or not."

As a player, Jim Pollard was a winner. In fact, he had won almost every honor that basketball could bestow upon a player. He was a college All-American, an AAU All-American,

Back row: Charlie Singley, Bob Ames, Bob Maples, Charlie Greenberg, Coach Jim Pollard. Front row: Frank Blachter, Fran O'Malley.

and a NBL, BAA, and NBA All-Star. In his only year as a collegian, Stanford won the NCAA title. In the AAU he led two teams to the finals. In six of his eight years with the Lakers, Minneapolis was crowned the champion.

Throughout his professional career, those who analyzed Pollard's performance tended to follow one of two well-worn paths. One was to examine his on court relationship with George Mikan. The two stars were so different that it was easier to contrast than to compare them. Max Winter finessed the issue best, perhaps, when he compared Mikan to Babe Ruth and Pollard to Ty Cobb. Mikan beat you with power, Pollard hurt you in any number of ways.

The second thread that fans and journalists often pursued was linked to Pollard's ability to do the spectacular. Because of his athleticism and creativity, writers and fans came to *expect* the sensational. Why couldn't he do the unusual all the time? However one wishes to answer this question, no one could doubt Jim Pollard's contributions to professional basketball in Minneapolis. Pollard, in turn, acknowledged his debt to professional basketball, admitting that there was "no other way I could have made the same amount of money and the same contacts. My only regret is that I'm growing old and have to get out."

In the summer of 1955, Jim and Arilee moved to Philadelphia for their next adventure, along with their children—Jack, who was seven, Jeanne, five, and Jeff, who was approaching one.

When Pollard met his new "family," the La Salle Explorers, six of the seven were veterans of the 1955 NCAA finals. The one person who was missing was Tom Gola, La Salle's great All-American. At 6' 6" Gola was almost a clone of Jim Pollard. He could play inside or outside. The most striking fact about the returning Explorers was that they were small. The tallest of the lot, Bob Maples, was 6' 5". In January Pollard got some size when 6' 8" Ed Givnich became eligible. And during the season La Salle posted a respectable 15-10 record. In Pollard's second year the team improved to 17-8. Anticipating even greater success in 1957-58, La Salle failed to live up to expectations and finished 15-9. Shortly afterwards, a disappointed Pollard resigned as La Salle's basketball coach.

In reflecting upon the experience, Pollard explained that "You can only get security in coaching at a school where there is a minimum of pressure. But then the financial

Jim at a benefit with YMCA executive Bob Allen (left), Phillie's pitcher Robin Roberts and Philadelphia Eagles' linebacker Tom Scott.

return isn't as great. With more pressure, naturally, there is more money but less security." Bob Vetrone, writing for Philadelphia's *Evening Bulletin*, wondered if Pollard's "biggest liability as a coach possibly was his inability to be mean to his players...."

Once the family had gotten their bearings in Philadelphia, Pollard lost little time taking up the same activities and community involvement that he had cultivated in Minneapolis. He spoke to civic organizations, church groups, and school groups. Friends in the world of athletics would call when they passed through town—everyone from Billy Martin, Vern Mikkleson and Bud Grant to Bob Griese, Don Shula, and Nate Thurmond.

Pollard was a family man, and when he wasn't on the road with the Explorers, he was home, doing family things. As his daughter Jeanne recalls:

> My folks were not "drop -'em off" folks, but "How can I help?" folks. They drove to all of our activities, stayed with

> us, supporting and cheering. Dad was an Indian Guide with my older brother, a timer for 10 years at the AAU-level competitive swimming meets my brothers and I participated in, a timer for my brothers track and cross-country teams, a coach for both of my brothers' baseball and basketball teams.

Not suprisingly, Pollard instilled a love of athletics in his children. His eldest son, Jack, played basketball, ran track and cross country, finishing fourth in the quarter-mile at the Illinois state track meet his senior year track. He earned All American honors at Mankato State University in south Minnesota and captained the team to an undefeated season.

Jeanne swam competitively for 10 years, was a multiple state winner, ran some track and cross country, sailed, and was a cheerleader. Jeff, the youngest, played football, basketball, and baseball, though eventually scuba diving became his life-long love.

Jim's wife Arilee was no slouch on the tennis court, either. But her main contribution to the Pollard sporting scene may have been as Jim's number one fan. As in the years in Minneapolis, she didn't miss a game, except on the occasions when young Pollards were born during the basketball season. In Minneapolis, Arilee had been active with the wives of the other players, networking, organizing showers, parties and get togethers, arranging help for new babies and generally supporting the women when the team was on the road. In Philadelphia, she began to devote greater energy to seeking out activities for her children, and eventually became a Scout leader, chairman of state swim meets, and local president of the Welcome Wagon. Family parties and gatherings at the Pollard home were the way of life, and anyone who didn't have a place for Sunday dinner or Thanksgiving was welcome there.

While at La Salle, Jim and Arilee worked at a YMCA camp in nearby Downing Town during the summer months. Bill Foster, a high school basketball coach, was the administrative assistant. He and Jim became good friends and decided to organize the Jim Pollard Coaches Clinic. It began as a one-day affair and evolved into a two-day clinic. They brought in coaches such as John Wooden, Ray Meyer, Frank McGuire, and Adolph Rupp. Foster remembered that Jim helped him get a head coaching job at Abington High School, a highly regarded school in the area. From there Foster went to Bloomsburg State, Rutgers, Utah, Duke, and Northwestern. Although Pollard and Foster moved in different directions, the clinic flourished and drew more than 500 coaches at its peak. After fourteen years, they sold the clinic to Scholastic Coach. Years later, Bill Foster remembered Pollard as "one of the most accessible and gracious former athletics that I had ever met."

After resigning from La Salle, the Pollard family returned to Minneapolis. Jim had a number of business opportunities and chose to sell cars for Oscar Borton, a close friend. While Pollard seemed uninterested in coaching, his name was bandied about for the top job with the Lakers. During Pollard's three-year sojourn at La Salle, the Lakers suffered three losing seasons and continued to struggle at the box office. In 1955-56 the Lakers finished 33-39, with George Mikan coming out of retirement in January 1956 to assist the struggling club. Mikan averaged 10.5 points in 37 games that season. Despite a losing record, the Lakers made the playoffs but were eliminated by the improving St. Louis Hawks. (Ben Kerner had moved the Hawks from Milwaukee to St. Louis in the summer of 1955.)

In 1956-57 the Lakers finished 34-38, in a three-way tie with St. Louis and Fort Wayne. In a round robin, the

The Coaches Clinic: from left, Jack Kraft of Malvern Prep, Fred Taylor from Ohio State, Harry Litwack of Temple, Ben Carnavale of Navy, Jim Pollard, Doug Connally of West Philadelphia, Bill Foster of Bloomington High School. (Bill Foster is past president of Naismith Basketball HOF and currently a member of its board of trustees.)

Pistons were eliminated and the Lakers faced the Hawks to determine who would represent the Western Division in the finals. Guiding the Hawks on the floor was Slater Martin. The fiery guard had been traded to the New York Knicks for Walter Dukes before the 1956-57 season. New York, in turn, had traded Martin to the Hawks for Willie Naulls. By 1956 Vern Mikkelsen was the sole link remaining to the Laker dynasty. The Hawks took the series 3-0, but the Lakers did not go down easily losing by two, 106-104, in St. Louis and in double overtime, 143-135, in Minneapolis.

In 1957 Ben Berger, frustrated that the city would not build a new arena for the Lakers, sold the team to a group of investors headed by local businessmen Bob Short and Frank Ryan. Pressured by the new management, George Mikan and John Kundla swapped jobs; Mikan became the coach, Kundla the general manager. Before the 1957-58 season began, Kundla traded Clyde Lovellette to the Cincinnati Royals for Ed Fleming and a number one draft choice, who turned out to be West Virginia's Hot Rod Hundley. The trade left the Lakers with Jim Krebs and Larry Foust at the center position. Weakened by the trade, the Lakers won only nine of their first thirty-nine games. On January 15 Mikan and Kundla traded places again, and the Lakers finished with an embarrassing 19-53 record.

For the first time in its history, Minneapolis was out of the playoffs. The franchise had hit rock bottom. The season's saving grace was that by finishing last, the Lakers had the first pick in the 1958 draft. Minneapolis did not botch this opportunity. The Lakers selected 6' 6" Elgin Baylor from Seattle University. At 225 pounds Baylor was not only a prolific scorer but a fierce rebounder. Noted for his bewildering hang time and acrobatic offensive moves, Baylor would be named to the All-NBA first team ten times. In 1958-59, Baylor led the Lakers to a 33-39 record which put them back in the playoffs. To the surprise of the experts, the Lakers eliminated Detroit and St. Louis to reach finals against the Boston Celtics. The Cinderella story ended when Boston took four straight from Minneapolis.

With arguably the most exciting player in the league, the Lakers future seemed bright, but trouble lay ahead. Vern Mikkelsen retired after the 1959 finals, leaving the Lakers without a veteran presence, and John Kundla, who had been with the organization from its inception, left the Lakers to take the head job at the University of Minnesota. The Lakers named John Castellani, Baylor's coach at Seattle, to replace him. Baylor entered the army, and could play only sporadically for the Lakers, and the team was 11 and 25 when Laker management decided to make a coaching change. On January 2, 1960 they called upon Jim Pollard to salvage the season.

For Pollard the experience started out with a bang. Two weeks after he had taken the position, the franchise barely escaped going down in flames. After a Sunday afternoon game on January 17 in St. Louis, the team climbed aboard its DC-3 for the return trip to Minneapolis, along with Jim's son Jack, three other children, and Frank Ryan, the team's attorney. Shortly after taking off the plane's generator died. Everything—lights, radio, navigation devices and heat—was dead. The plane's pilot, Vernon Ullman, thought it too risky to return to St. Louis's Lambert Field so, flying by the stars, he headed north toward Minneapolis. Under normal conditions, the return flight was two hours. After three and a half hours, the plane, covered with ice and out of fuel, was nowhere near Minneapolis. Miraculously, Ullman spotted a cornfield near Carroll, Iowa, and landed the plane as light as a feather. None of the 20 passengers and flight crew were injured. Happy to be alive, the Lakers counted their blessings and looked forward to the rest of the season.

During the evacuation, Pollard had calmly got everyone else off the plane into cars. When the last car came to pick him up, he realized how nearly they had come to disaster. The car was a hearse.

Pollard's impact on the team's attitude was more significant than on its win-loss record. The team finished the season at 25 wins and 50 losses. Pollard's record of 14 wins and 25 losses was only marginally better than Castellani's 11 and 25, but Pollard had settled the team down and snuffed out the dissension that was developing under Castellani. There were also some player personnel changes. Seeking more size, the Lakers traded Dick Garmaker to the New York Knicks for

6' 11" Ray Felix. Minneapolis then swapped veteran centers, sending Larry Foust to St. Louis for Charley Share. Despite the dismal season, the Lakers managed to hang on to third place in the Western Division, which put them in the playoffs once again. Then the Lakers got hot. They took two in a row from the Detroit Pistons, which put them in the finals against St. Louis. In a short series it was possible that the Lakers could ride Baylor's back to the finals. He also had some help. Rudy LaRusso was a talented forward, Frank Selvy, a big guard who could shoot, Bob Leonard, a veteran guard, and Rod Hundley, whose antics off the court had given management fits, was another solid guard. Ray Felix started at center and Jim Krebs, Boo Ellis and Tom Hawkins helped off the bench. The Lakers had eliminated St. Louis in 1959 and almost did it again in 1960. After five games the Lakers had a 3-2 edge and a chance to close out the series in the sixth game at Minneapolis. Instead, the Hawks prevailed in Minneapolis and took the seventh game in St. Louis. Although the regular season had been a disappointment, Pollard and his players could take come satisfaction from their playoff run.

Overshadowing the team's performance, in 1959-60, was the looming reality that the Lakers were about to leave Minneapolis. Bob Short and Frank Ryan were losing money and wanted to take the club to Los Angeles. The Lakers had not drawn particularly well even in their glory years and the losing seasons added to their financial woes. On February 9, Halsey Hall of the *Minnesota Star* quoted owner Short as saying: "The response of Los Angeles has been overwhelming."

Because of the travel costs for other teams, Short worried that the NBA's board of governors might not approve the move. His concern proved to be well-founded. On the morning of April 27, the owners denied his request. Then dumb luck smiled on Short. On the 26th Abe Saperstein announced that he was about to organize a competing professional league, the American Basketball League. If the NBA did not approve his request, Short could jump to the new league. The owners reconsidered their vote, and the Lakers packed their bags for Los Angeles and its 14,000-seat Sports Arena. Though it disappointed die-hard fans in Minnesota, it was far from unusual at the time. Of the eight teams that opened the NBA's 1954-55 season, four had moved to new markets by 1960. Milwaukee had moved to St. Louis in 1955, Fort Wayne to Detroit in 1956, and Rochester to Cincinnati in 1956.

The Laker's future on the court began to look brighter when, following Pollard's recommendation, they drafted Jerry West with the second pick in the first round of the 1960 NBA draft. An All-American at West Virginia University, West soon joined teammate Baylor as a perennial All-NBA player. This exciting one-two punch would revive the Lakers claim to being one of the most successful franchises in NBA history.

To coach the team the Lakers tapped Fred Schaus, an NBA veteran who had coached West and Hundley at West Virginia. If there was any disappointment for the Lakers, it was that they simply could not beat the Celtics in the six times they met for the NBA championship during the 1960s. This rivalry, however, solidified the NBA's place as a major sport in the United States. For Bob Short and Frank Ryan the move proved to be an excellent investment. In 1965 they sold the Lakers for $5,175,000 in cash to Jack Kent Cooke.

Pollard returned to his job selling cars for Oscar Borton, but his brief stint as an NBA coach had not dulled his interest in coaching. In 1961 the NBA returned to Chicago for the first time since 1950, and Max Winter, the Lakers original

The Chicago Packers

general manager, was associated with the Chicago ownership group headed by Dave Trager. On February 23, 1961, the new team announced that Jim Pollard had signed a two-year contract in the $20,000 range to coach the team. Home games were to be played in Chicago's International Amphitheater in the heart of Chicago's stockyards. Influenced by the location, the team's nickname was the Packers.

As an expansion team, the NBA awarded Chicago the first choice in the draft. Jim drafted Walt Bellamy, a 6' 11" well-proportioned center from the University of Indiana, who had played on the 1960 Olympic team. While Bellamy earned rookie of the year honors and averaged 31.6 points a game, second to Wilt Chamberlain, he had a weak supporting cast. The Packers finished 18-62 and fired Pollard at the end of the season. For the 1962-63 season the team moved to the Chicago Coliseum and changed its name to the Zephyrs. The following year the franchise moved to Baltimore. NBA basketball did not return to Chicago until 1966 with the Chicago Bulls.

For the next five years Jim Pollard was essentially out of

basketball. He and his family lived in Mt. Prospect, Illinois, where Jim worked in sales and Arilee continued to teach. Jim's one connection with basketball was as a color commentator for Loyola University basketball games alongside Red Rush, a popular Chicago announcer.

As a result of that assocation, the Pollard family and the Rush family became good friends. Jim valued Red's friendship highly, because the affection was genuine, and not a product of his celebrity. The two families spent holidays together and the children mixed well. One Thanksgiving, young Jeff Pollard and Casey Rush happened upon one of Red's cigars. Being kids, they wanted to know what the hoopla was about, so they decided the smoke it out in the back yard. Jim and Red discovered their sons puffing away. As Jeff Pollard tells it:

Dad said to Red that he was so excited that his son finally was going to smoke, and encouraged me to finish it off. Red demonstrated how you inhale it and hold it, but he told us we had to finish the whole thing off to be successful.

Both children lost their dinners in the course of the experiment … and neither smoked as adults.

On February 2, 1967, Jim Pollard jumped back into the world of basketball when George Mikan stood at the podium at New York's Summit Hotel to announce to a group of investors and promoters the creation of the American Basketball Association. One of the eleven teams in the new league was the Minnesota Muskies, and Pollard would be the coach. The centerpiece of the team was Mel Daniels, a 6' 9" All-American from the University of New

Mexico. Other key players were Les Hunter, a 6' 7" forward who started on Loyola's 1963 NCAA championship team, Don Freeman, a guard, and Skip Thoren, a center, both of whom stared at the University of Illinois. Sam Smith from Kentucky Wesleyan was a 6' 7" forward and Errol Palmer, was a 6' 5" forward from DePaul. Erv Inniger from Indiana, Ron Perry from Virginia Tech, and Terry Kunze from Minnesota were the other guards, and Gary Keller of the University of Florida and Dick Clark of Eastern Kentucky were also on the team.

The Muskies finished the season just behind the Pittsburgh Pipers with a 50-28 record—the second-best in the league. In the first round of the playoffs they eliminated the Kentucky Colonels, but the Pipers, led by Connie Hawkins, Charlie Williams, and Art Heyman, were too much for them and took the semifinal playoff, 4 games to 1.

For Pollard the season was extremely satisfying. Jim Kaplan of the *Minneapolis Star*, described the season as a "vindication for the quiet man." Despite the ups and downs of his coaching career, Kaplan observed that Pollard "always played the nice guy role." The team had a great attitude, and Kaplan thought, "eliciting that attitude was Pollard's job."

Jim coached the All-Star team because the Muskies were in first place at the half way mark. From left: Fred Lewis, Les Hunter, Bob Netolicky, Coach Jim Pollard, Mel Daniels, Roger Brown, Don Freeman.

Coach Pollard on the bench with Muskies Dan Sparks and Irv Inniger.

In 1967-68 Minnesota's team cohesiveness was no small achievement. Between 1962, when Pollard left the Packers, and 1967, when he took the job with the Muskies, American society was rocked by turmoil. The civil rights movement, protests against the war in Vietnam, and riots in American cities left Americans divided and perplexed.

The sports world was not isolated from these larger events. Controversy swirled around Muhammad Ali and an effort by some African Americans to boycott the 1968 Olympics. When the Muskies were on the road, Jim Kaplan reported, Pollard assigned roommates and even taxis on an integrated basis. Kaplan thought this arrangement contributed to a good working relationship among the players. Race played a role, Kaplan thought, in contributing to the team's low attendance, given the reality that the Twin Cities were over 95 percent white and the Muskies did not have a white star. The Muskies

In 1969 Jim and Arilee celebrated their 25th wedding anniversary with children Jeanne, Jack, and Jeff.

drew an average of 2,400 for the season, 1,100 below the 3,500 needed to break even. Muskies management reported that it lost almost $500,000. In May Larry Shields, the team's majority stockholder and president, announced that he hoped to sell 450,000 shares of stock at one dollar a share. In April the Muskies had named Vern Mikkelsen the team's new general manager. By mid-May, however, the team announced it would move south to become the Miami Floridians.

In Miami Pollard assumed the duties of both general manager and coach. Strapped for cash, Shields decided to sell Mel Daniels to Indiana, but the other players, including Don Freeman, Irv Inniger, Ron Perry, Gary Keller, Les Hunter, and Skip Thoren, accompanied Pollard to Miami. Pollard's hope was that Don Sidle from Oklahoma, the team's first draft choice, would fill in the gap left by Daniels' departure.

Pollard made a good first impression on the media. Edwin Pope, sports editor of *The Miami Herald*, described him as "extroverted, articulate, energetic, and truthful." He added: "The latter attribute is not universal among professional coaches of any kind." While Pope was probably the first writer who ever described Pollard as "extroverted," the other adjectives certainly rang true.

The Floridians started slowly that year, winning only 11 of their first 28 games. As usual, Pollard didn't panic. His style was never to rant or rave during or after games. He explained: "If I hold it down I can talk to my team better during time-outs...." Pollard's patience paid off, as the team began to put together a series of winning streaks. The Floridians finished the season with a very respectable 43-35 record, one game behind the Indianapolis Pacers. In the first round of the playoffs, Miami eliminated the Minnesota Pipers, 4-3, but in the Eastern Division finals, they fell to the Indianapolis Pacers, 4-1. While the Floridians had been a success on the floor in their first season, as expected, they lost money at the gate.

Unfortunately for Pollard, the 1969-70 season got off to another bad start. At the end of November, the Floridians were in the Eastern Division cellar with a 5-15 record. Moreover, two of the team's stars, Don Freeman and Skip Thoren, were injured. When 1,621 showed up for a game against Indiana, Jim Huber, of the *Miami News* called the attendance "surprisingly high." On November 28, the Floridians fired Jim Pollard.

In responding to questions from the press, Pollard stated: "When you're losing you must do something. I'm disappointed but not shocked." In a little over two seasons, Pollard had compiled a respectable 98-78 record. The ABA franchise that he guided would never have a winning record again. After the 1972 season the Floridians went out of business. In 1975 the ABA ceased to exist, though four of the teams joined the NBA. Perhaps Bob Frisk, sports editor for Paddock Publications, summed it up best: "Isn't it amazing how a coach can be praised so highly at the end of one season and fired after just a few games of the next campaign. Such is the life of a coach in professional sports. Can there be a more insecure way of making a buck?"

In the fall of 1971, Fort Lauderdale University (FLU), a small private institution, hired Jim Pollard as its director of athletics, basketball coach, and fundraiser. After two years, FLU dropped its basketball program for financial reasons and Pollard left the university. For the next five years Jim taught high school social studies in Fort Lauderdale, and during that time he also found time to earn a master's degree at Florida Atlantic University. But basketball was never quite out of his blood, nor his willingness to help old friends. Ed Carroll had been an official at Jim's first game as a coach at LaSalle, and in 1971, Pollard and Carroll reconnected in Fort Lauderdale. Carroll had become the secretary-treasurer of the Broward County Opportunity Center which provided educational opportunities for children with learning disabilities, and he was organizing a high school basketball all-star game to raise money for the center. When Carroll asked Pollard to coach one of the teams, Jim readily agreed. Since Bob Davies, the former Rochester Royals star, lived in Florida, Jim asked him to coach the other team. For the next seven years these old rivals donated their time for a good cause.

In 1978 the Pollards returned to California. After several unsuccessful efforts to land a position as an athletic director, Jim worked for a year at the California Youth Authority in Stockton, and for the next eight years he taught physical education at Lodi Middle School and Delta Sierra Middle School. He had been active in the church throughout his adult life, and in Lodi he attended St. Paul's Lutheran Church and also served as a deacon.

Jim Pollard took his teaching responsibilities seriously. Judy McKelvy, one of his colleagues, remembered: "Everyone liked him, kids, faculty, parents. But he was no push-over. The kids knew that they had to mind their p's and q's. Jim would tolerate no nonsense where education was concerned." Another colleague, Wendy Coe, remembered that Jim loved to debate the issues faced by teachers whether it was the conduct of students or the performance of the administration. She said: "If you never had a debate with Jim, you really missed something." Although Jim's colleagues knew about his athletic achievements, they were also struck by his modesty. Judy McKelvey noted that Jim was never boastful or arrogant, and David Holmes, a counselor at Lodi Middle School, observed of Jim: "If you liked him, it was fine. If you didn't that was fine too. But you had better make sure the student's interests came first in (your) priorities. Then you were OK with him."

Jim with Don Barksdale

Just as Jim Pollard had helped out Ed Carroll in the 1970s, he assisted another old friend, Don Barksdale, in the 1980s. Barksdale, who grew up in Berkeley, California, and played for UCLA in 1947, was the first African American named to an All-America basketball team. In 1947-48, when Pollard signed with the Lakers, Barksdale replaced him as the star of the Oakland Bittners. In 1948, Barksdale was the first African-American to play on a United States Olympic basketball team. In his four-year NBA career (1952-55), Barksdale earned the distinction of being the first African American to play in an NBA All-Star Game (1953). In the 1980s, as funds dried up for high school sports in the Bay Area, Barksdale, who had gone on from his athletic career to become a successful businessman, conceived of the idea of raising money by hosting a Celebrity Waiters Benefit. Jim Pollard was one of the celebrities Barksdale could always count on to give a helping hand.

On May 1st, 1978, Jim Pollard enjoyed his greatest honor, when he was inducted in the Basketball Hall of

At the Enshrinement Ceremonies at the Naismith Basketball Hall of Fame, May 1, 1978: Cliff Hagen, Joe Fulks Jr. (for his father), John Nucatola, Jim Pollard, Paul Arizin.

Jim Pollard (left) at the Bay Area Sports Hall of Fame, Feb. 17, 1989 with George Blanda, Maye Lazzeri (for her husband Tony), John Naber and Willie Stargell.

Fame in Springfield, Massachusetts. In 1989 the Bay Area Hall of Fame and the Stanford University Hall of Fame also honored him. But the growing collection of honors did nothing to swell his head. Whether Jim was attending a reunion of Oakland Technical High School or an enshrinement ceremony at the Basketball Hall of Fame, he was the same person. Frank Isola, a high school baseball teammate and lifelong friend, remembered that Jim had the ability to make "you feel so important." Although Jim was a celebrity, Isola added: "He never forgot his roots and was always loyal to his old friends."

In 1990 Jim Pollard retired from the Lodi public schools. During his last school year Jim had his gall bladder removed. By 1992, he was fighting Waldenstrom macroglobulinemia, a cousin to leukemia, and experiencing all the side effects of chemotherapy. In the summer of 1992 Jim and Arilee decided to travel across the county to see old friends and their sons Jack and Jeff. One of the stops was in Minnesota, where the Lakers had a reunion organized by Whitey Skoog. Not long after this trip, on January 22, 1993, Jim Pollard died at the age of seventy.

In a poll taken during his years with the Lakers, Jim Pollard was selected by his peers as the best player of the league's early history, and in 1963 the Academy of Sports Editors named him one of the ten members of the "All-Time NBA Team." Others on the list included Bob Cousy, Bill Russell, George Mikan, Elgin Baylor, Wilt Chamberlain, Oscar Robertson, Bob Pettit, Dolph Schayes, and Paul Arizin.

Jim and Arilee at the Hall of Fame

Thirty years later, in 1996, when the NBA named its top fifty players, Jim Pollard's name was not on the list. In 1999 Hall of Fame coach Alex Hannum, wrote: "To this day, I cannot understand how one of the top ten players ever to play the game could be overlooked." Bob Cousy once remarked: "Jim was the best forward of his time and one of ten or twelve players they overlooked when voting for the top 50. He was by far the most athletic of the big guys in those days…."

What this demonstrates is that by any standard, athletic fame is a fleeting commodity. The biggest test for most athletes is how they handle their lives when the cheering stops. David Holmes, a colleague at Lodi Middle School, may have captured Jim Pollard best when he wrote: "Besides being a professional basketball player, he was a professional teacher." From the playgrounds of Oakland to the schoolyards of Lodi, Jim Pollard pushed himself, his teammates, his players, and his students to strive for excellence. Beginning on those playgrounds, Jim Pollard also developed the gift of caring for others and making those around him feel important. Those who had the pleasure of watching Jim Pollard play basketball recognized him as a unique talent. And those who knew him off the court were always struck by his special grace.

INDEX

A

Adams, Cedric 77
Ajax, Warren 45, 51
Alameida, Bob 37
Ali, Muhammad 163
Allen, Bob 152
Anderson, Clarence "Swede" 20
Andrews, Jack 135
Arizin, Paul 108, 122, 123, 168, 170
Auerbach, Arnold "Red" 72, 73

B

Barker, Cliff 78
Barksdale, Don 167–168
Baylor, Elgin 156, 158, 159, 170
Beahon, George 53, 54, 93
Beard, Ralph 78, 92, 109
Bee, Clair 62
Bellamy, Walt 160
Bennett, Carl 124
Berger, Ben 43-5, 67, 86, 89, 90, 105, 155
Berger, Midge 89
Biasone, Danny 86, 134, 135, 138, 141
Bittner, Lou 37
Blanda, George 169
Borgia, Sid 77, 119
Borton, Oscar 154, 159
Boryla, Vince 8, 76, 96, 114-116, 118, 126
Brachman, Bob 39
Braun, Carl 118, 126
Brian, Frank 125

Brown, Roger 162
Browning, Bud 39
Bunn, John 23
Burness, Don 23-5, 37
Burnett, Bob 138

C

Cahn, Leonard 35
Calhoun, Bill 8, 37, 61, 65, 66
Callahan, John 19, 20
Cann, Howard 69, 70, 118
Carberry, Jack 30
Carlson, Bill 52, 54, 109, 143
Carlson, Don "Swede" 43, 45, 48, 73
Carpenter, Gordon 35, 36
Carroll, Ed 166-7
Castellani, John 156
Cervi, Al 61, 62, 64-6, 86, 87, 118, 134-7
Chalfen, Morris 43, 44
Chamberlain, Wilt 160, 170
Christgau, John 55, 56, 58
Clark, Dick 162
Clifton, Nat "Sweetwater" 60, 85, 95, 97, 116
Cobb, Ty 150
Coe, Wendy 167
Coleman, Jack 93, 94, 133
Connelley, Tee 34
Conroy, Ed 29
Conti, Al 31
Cooke, Jack Kent 159
Cooper, Chuck 94, 95
Cousy, Bob 56, 83, 117, 122, 123, 131, 133, 134, 144, 170
Cowden, Bill 23, 24

Cowles, Ozzie 26, 83, 103
Cox, Verdie 28
Crowe, George 60
Cullum, Dick 76, 110, 111
Cumberland, Roscoe 60

D

Dallmar, Howie 23, 24, 26, 31, 139
Dana, Jack 24, 26
Daniels, Mel 161, 162, 164
Davidson, Kenny 24
Davies, Bobby 62, 64, 66, 97, 108, 109, 122, 123, 147, 166
Davis, Hal 78
Dean, Everett 23, 24, 26, 139
De Grazia, Emilio 8
Dewey, Governor Tom 127
Dorsey, Tommy 27
Douglas, Robert J 60
Drexler, Clyde 11
Dropo, Mel 29
Duffy, Bob 20
Dukes, Walter 155
Duncan, Andy 35, 65
Durkee, Bill 42, 43, 51
Dwan, Jack 51

E

Effrat, Louis 119
Ellis, Boo 158
Ellison, Pervis 68
Embry, R.C. 39
Excel, Ken 45, 51

F

Farrar, Harry 21

Feerick, Bob 29, 73
Felix, Ray 158
Ferrin, Arnie 35, 67, 68, 70-2, 74, 81, 84, 88, 90, 92, 105, 144
Filiberti, Ernie 31
Finney, Peter 145
Fisher, Mickey 69
Fleming, Ed 156
Forman 70, 71
Forman, Don 8, 67, 69, 70, 71, 77
Foster, Bill 154
Foust, Larry 98, 125, 144, 147, 156, 158
Frantsen, Myer 102
Frazier, Walt 113
Freeman, Don 162, 164, 165
Frisk, Bob 166
Fulks, Joe Jr. 122, 168

G

Gabor, Billy 86, 134
Gaff, Glen 72-3, 118-9, 132, 135
Gallatin, Harry 89, 96, 113, 115, 116, 126
Gardner, Jack 104
Garmaker, Dick 157
Gates, William "Pop" 60
Geen, Al 22, 27
Gerber, Bob 48, 51
Givnich, Ed 151
Gola, Tom 148, 151
Gottlieb, Leo 115
Grant, Bud 86, 98, 152
Gray, Jack 80

173

Green, Ben 55
Griese, Bob 152
Griffith, Eddie 34
Groza, Alex 35, 78, 108, 109, 123
Gruenig, Robert 22, 35, 36

H

Hagan, Cliff 143, 168
Hall, Halsey 158
Hanger, Chuck 29
Hanham, Homer 82
Hannin, Harry 37
Hannum, Alex 35, 86, 170
Hansen, Banna Alma 32
Hansen, William 32
Harris, Bob 116, 135
Harrison, Bob 8, 76, 78, 81-4, 87, 88, 02, 105, 107, 110, 121, 125, 131, 133, 137, 147
Harrison, Jack 60, 67
Harrison, Les 37, 60-3, 92, 96, 98, 107, 133, 147
Hartkopf, "Baldy" 99
Hartman, Sid 43-6, 48, 90, 110
Hawkins, Connie 162
Hawkins, Tom 158
Hayes, Gayle 34
Haynes, Marques 56, 70, 71, 85
Heff, Art 133
Hendrickson, Joe 41, 52-4, 75, 110
Hermsen, Kleggie 73
Hertzberg, Sonny 73
Heyman, Art 162
Hickey, Nat 63, 64

Hillsman, Ralph 20
Hitch, Lew 8, 103, 104, 125, 130, 146, 147
Hogan, Frank 95
Holland, Joe 78
Holmes, David 167, 171
Holstein, Jim 8, 122, 128, 129
Holzman, "Red" 63, 66, 93
Houbregs, Bob 147
Huber, Jim 165
Hundley 156, 158, 159
Hundley, Hot Rod 156, 158, 159
Hunter, Les 162, 164
Hutchins, Mel 147
Hutton, Joe 46, 81, 90, 102, 104, 105, 110, 125
Hutton, Joe Jr. 46, 79, 89, 102, 110

I

Inniger, Erv 162, 164
Irish, Ned 51, 78, 95, 96, 112, 114, 115, 117, 133
Irving, Julius 84
Irwin, Nelson "Doc" 114
Isola, Frank 169

J

Jaros, Tony 43, 45, 71, 72, 80, 81, 86, 88, 105
Johnson, Arnie 64
Johnson, Charles 65, 101, 143
Johnson, Fon 34
Jones, "Wah Wah" 78
Jordan, Michael 11, 26, 84
Julian, Doggie 134

K

Kaftan, George 83, 118
Kalafat, Ed 143
Kaplan, Jim 163
Karch, Augie 147, 148
Keller, Gary 162, 164
Kempter, Richard 46
Kerner, Ben 154
King, Dolly 57
King, George 134, 136
King, Wilbert 56
Koehler, Ray 15, 19, 26, 27
Koppett, Leonard 112, 119, 127
Krebs, Jim 156, 158
Krishef, Robert K. 45
Kundla, Anna 46
Kundla, John 8, 46-8, 51, 52, 66, 70, 71, 82, 84, 88, 90, 93, 120-122, 131-142 passim, 156
Kundla, John Sr. 46
Kunze, Terry 162
Kurland, Bob 38, 39
Kyte, Al 15, 16

L

Lapchick, Joe 96, 97, 112, 113, 116, 118, 120, 122, 129
LaRusso, Rudy 158
Lazzeri, Maye 169
Lazzeri, Tony 169
Leonard, Bob 158
Levane, Andy "Fuzzy" 97
Lewis, Fred 162
Linari, Fred 25-27
Lloyd, Earl 95, 134, 135

Loeffler, Ken 148
Lonborg, Dutch 55
Lovellette, Clyde 130, 135, 143, 145, 146, 148, 156
Lubin, Frank 35
Luisetti, Hank 15, 23, 24, 29, 30, 31, 38, 102
Lumpp 119
Lumpp, Ray 118

M

Macauley, Ed 70, 122, 134
Macknowski, Johnny 86
MacMillan, Dave 45, 47, 103
Maples, Bob 151
Martin, Billy 152
Martin, Slater (Duggy) 8, 78, 80-3, 85, 88, 93, 102, 102, 108-9, 119-21, 125-6, 129, 131-2, 138, 143-5, 148, 152, 155
Masters, Al 139
Matson, Ellis 47
Mattei, Paul 50
McBurney, Ross 19
McCaffrey, Leo 14, 15, 23, 26
McCarty, Tom 34
McCracken, Jack 22
McGovern, Ray 36
McGowen, Deane 128
McGuire, Al 118, 119, 126
McGuire, Dick 8, 96, 113, 114, 126
McGuire, Frank 154
McGuire, John and Winnifred 113
McKelvy, Judy 167
McKinney, Horace 73

175

McNamee, Joe 94
McNatt, Jim "Scat" 35
Meineke, Don 125
Meitz, Ken 20, 22
Mendell, Robert 8
Meyer, Ray 50, 120, 154
Mikan, Ed 50
Mikan, George 9, 11, 12, 41, 49, 50-4, 58-60, 63, 64, 66, 67, 69, 70-75, 77, 81, 83-90, 92, 93, 95, 98, 101, 102, 104, 105-110, 119-138 passim, 143, 147, 150, 154-6, 161, 170
Mikan, Joseph 50
Mikan, Minne 50
Mikkelsen 8, 46, 78-81, 85, 87, 92-5, 104-110, 120-147 passim, 155-6, 164
Miller, Melvin 19, 21, 22
Mitchell, Wes 46
Molinas, Jack 142
Monasch, Burton 69-70
Moore, Bobby 13, 16, 18, 22
Mortola, Bill 34

N

Naber, John 169
Napolitano, Paul 29, 31, 37, 42, 43, 49
Naulls, Willie 155
Neal, Jim 137
Needham, Roy 80
Neff, Bennie 23, 65
Nelson, Chet 28, 30, 35-6, 39
Netolicky, Bob 162
Nichols, Jack 73
Norlander, John 79

Nucatola, John 168

O

O'Brien, Gene 99
O'Malley, Joe 29
O'Shea, Kevin 31, 80, 81, 89, 90
Osterkorn, Wally 134

P

Paine, Alva 34
Palmer, Bud 115
Palmer, Errol 162
Payak, Johnny 82
Perry, Ron 162, 164
Peterson, Jim 66
Peterson, Vadal 67
Pettit, Bob 145, 170
Phillip, Andy 35, 72, 117, 125, 147
Pippin, Scotty 11
Pitts 40
Pitts, R.C. 39
Podoloff, Maurice 42, 67, 98, 107, 117, 133, 137, 140, 142
Pollard, Arilee 7, 8, 31, 32, 33, 37, 38, 48, 49, 74, 75, 76, 77, 90, 139, 149, 151, 153, 154, 161, 164, 169, 170
Pollard, Gus 13
Pollard, Jim
  baseball career 98-100
  Chicago Packers (coach) 160-61
  childhood 13-15
  Coast Guard 28-31
  courtship 31-33
  Floridians (coach) 164-66

Pollard, Jim (cont)
   Golden State Creamery
     (AAU) 18-22
   Hall of Fame, 168-9
   high school years 15-18
   Lakers (coach) 157-9
   Lakers 41-111, 120-148,
   later career 166-171
   move to Mpls 48
   Oakland Bittners 37-40
   reputation 11-12, 123, 170-71
   San Diego Dons 34-36
   Stanford 22-27

Pollard, Esther 13
Pollard, Jack 91, 151, 153, 157, 164, 170
Pollard, Jeanne 8, 18, 75, 151, 152, 153, 164
Pollard, Jeff 151, 161, 164, 170
Pollard, Ruth 13
Pollard, Susie 13, 23, 33
Pollard, Tom 13
Pope, Edwin 165
Pressley, "Babe" 56, 85

R

Ratkovicz, George 64, 86
Reddy, Bill 131
Reed, Willis 113
Renick, Jesse 35, 36
Rice, William T. 34
Risen, Arnie 8, 10, 54, 63-5, 94, 95, 108, 144
Roberts, Robin 152
Robertson, Oscar 170
Robinson, Ermer 56, 59, 85

Robinson, Jackie 57
Rock, Gene 13, 14, 22
Rocker, John 42, 43, 48, 51
Roehling, Sharon 8
Roos, Harry 34
Rupp, Adolph 154
Rush, Casey 161
Rush, Red 161
Russell, Bill 170
Russell, John "Honey" 62
Ruth, Babe 50, 150
Ryan, Frank 155, 157-9

S

Sailors, Kenny 35
Saperstein 31, 55, 56, 58, 107, 159
Saperstein, Abe 31, 159
Saul, Frank "Pep" 106, 110, 119, 121, 125, 129, 131, 143
Schaefer, Herm 51, 52, 71, 73, 82, 84, 88, 108
Schaus, Fred 125, 159
Schayes, Dolph 70, 86, 134, 135, 136, 170
Schnittker, Dick 130
Schultz, Howie 8, 46, 64, 76, 79, 104, 125, 130
Schwartz, Ray 16, 18
Scolari, Fred 29, 35, 73, 125-6
Scott, Tom 152
Seltz, Rollie 79
Selvy, Frank 158
Seymour, Paul 82, 86, 87, 88, 134, 135, 136, 137
Share, Charlie 125, 158
Sharman, Bill 134

177

Sheppard, Mrs. J.H. 80
Short, Bob 155, 158, 159
Shula, Don 152
Sidle, Don 164
Silver, Morris 29
Singley, Charlie 150
Simmons, Connie 97, 117, 120, 121
Sinatra, Frank 27
Skoog, Myer "Whitey" 8, 102, 103, 106, 128, 129, 131, 148, 170
Smith, Don 45, 48
Smith, Sam 162
Spears, Odie 110
Stargell, Willie 169
Sunderlage, Don 143

T

Tanenbaum, Sid 43, 70
Tatum, Reese "Goose" 56, 85
Taulbee, Warren 37
Thoren, Skip 162, 164, 165
Thurmond, Nate 152
Todorovich, Marko 66
Towery, Blackie 90
Trager, Dave 160
Truman, President Harry 57

U

Uline, Mike 72
Ullman, Vernon 157

V

Vance, Gene 72
Vandeweghe, Ernie 97, 117, 118, 126, 127

Vetrone, Bob 152
Voss, Ed 23

W

Wanzer, Bobby 8, 35, 62-4, 108, 123, 144
Ward, Arch 55
Weir, Bob 20, 21, 22
West, Jerry 159
Wheatley, Bill 20, 21, 22, 37, 40
White, Maurice 48
Wilkinson, Dorr 82
Williams, Charlie 162
Williams, Don 24, 37, 38
Winston, Morris 44
Winter, Max 43, 44, 54, 55, 58, 79, 80, 88, 106, 107, 126, 131, 136, 138, 150, 159
Winter, Tex 104
Wood, Hal 29
Wooden, John 154

Y

Yardley, George 132, 144, 147

Z

Zaslofsky, Max 72, 97, 117, 121, 123
Ziegenfuss, George 31
Zollner, Fred 124
Zollner, Theodore 124